ibunka!

www.ibunka.jp

Stephen Richmond

Bruno Vannieu

www.almalang.com

Intercultural communication in language classes?

We tried for many years to introduce some basic ideas about intercultural communication in our own foreign language classes, but found that this was quite difficult.

Looking back, we see that there were two basic reasons behind our struggle.

- One reason was that we were trying to introduce **concepts** such as *individualism, non-verbal communication*, or *perception*, but realized that students found it difficult to relate to such abstract notions.

- Another stumbling block was that our **students had difficulties expressing themselves** in English about culture and cultural differences. This was a big problem for us, because we are both first and foremost foreign language teachers, and we needed our classes to be interactive.

Over time, trial and error in the classroom led us to two conclusions:

❶ We should begin by having students reflect on their own lifestyles and opinions, and following that, look at other cultural realities through the prism of **everyday life**. In short, to help students broaden their worldview, we must meet them where they are in terms of life experience.

❷ We must provide **resources for guided expression** (and provide language support to aid comprehension when necessary) to help students **speak about culture with nuance**.

Ibunka! is the result of putting these ideas onto the page, and having many generous people share their thoughts and experiences through the *Ibunka Survey*. We hope you and your students find it both stimulating and fun.

-The Authors

LANGUAGE LEARNING

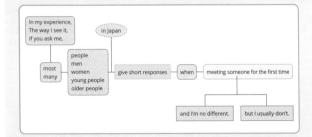

The core target of this textbook is **intermediate-level EFL students** with **basic conversational ability**. For them, the next challenge is to <u>learn to speak with nuance</u> and <u>express their opinions rationally</u>:

- **qualifying what they say** - for example by saying "Many elderly Japanese people like to..." instead of "Japanese people like to..."

- **expressing their personal habits and points of view in relation to their society's values:** "Most university students in Japan... but personally..."

- **reacting respectfully to differences** by explaining what they find to be and why: "I found this to be surprising because..."

LEARNING ABOUT CULTURE

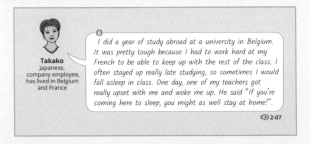

This book won't teach students all the theories of intercultural communication, or even give many definitive answers. But we hope it will help them to:

- develop an investigative, curious frame of mind

- realize that culture is a mosaic (for example, there are **considerable differences among Western countries**, which are sometimes lumped together from a Japanese perspective)

- get an idea of how cultural differences influence aspects of daily life, even within their own society

- understand a major reason why studying foreign languages is interesting and important.

CONTENTS

HOW TO USE THIS BOOK

CORE MATERIAL
6 pages x 11 units / pp. 8 ~ 73

Part 1

You and Your Culture

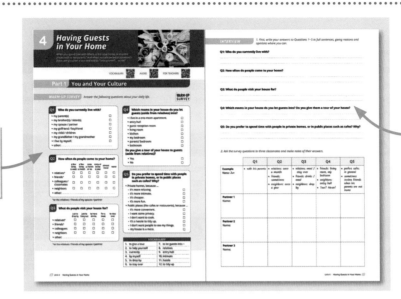

WARM-UP SURVEY
Fill out the survey as a quick way to start thinking about the topic.

INTERVIEW
Interview your classmates and take note of their answers (in the classroom or in online breakout rooms).

Part 2

People in Other Cultures

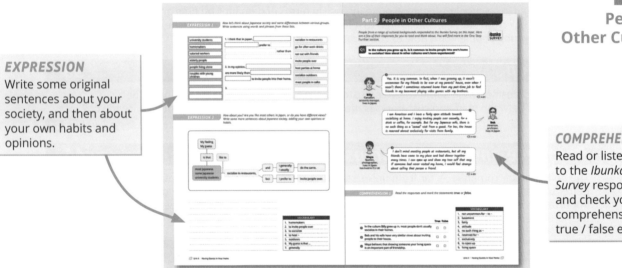

EXPRESSION
Write some original sentences about your society, and then about your own habits and opinions.

COMPREHENSION 1
Read or listen to the *Ibunka Survey* responses, and check your comprehension with true / false exercises.

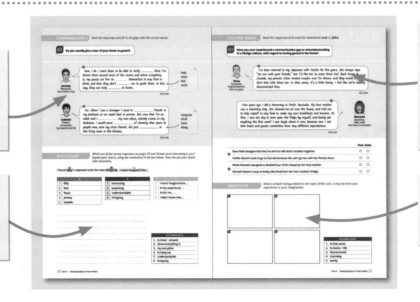

COMPREHENSION 2
Read or listen to the *Ibunka Survey* responses, and check your comprehension with gap-fill exercises.

DISCUSSION
Next, write your reaction to one of the responses, and discuss with classmates.

CULTURE SHOCK
Read or listen to the *Ibunka Survey* responses, and check your comprehension with true/false exercises.

CREATIVITY
Finally, create a simple manga (optional activity).

OPTIONAL MATERIAL

2 pages x 11 units / pp. 74 ~ 95

One Step Futher

For **more capable or motivated students**, the *One Step Further* sections provide extra survey responses and a guided activity that helps them look deeper into these responses to find evidence of cultural systems.

CULTURAL PATTERNS

Cultural habits can be grouped into general categories. Read and discuss the cultural patterns outlined here.

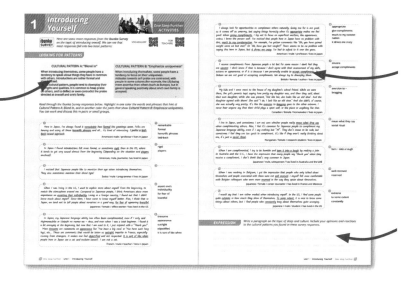

LOOKING FOR PATTERNS

Read through these extra *Ibunka Survey* responses, looking for words and phrases which reflect contrasting cultural patterns. Highlight them in different colors.

EXPRESSION

Write a short paragraph about the topic of this unit (optional activity).

Student Tutorial

Here is a short visual presentation that will walk you through the textbook, and show you how each part works.

TUTORIAL
A step-by-step guide on how to use this book

English

Japanese

RESOURCES FOR TEACHERS

Of course, this textbook can be used on its own, in a traditional classroom setting. However, several online and printed resources are available to make teachers' lives easier.

DIGITAL TEXTBOOK

The textbook is available in digital format:

- for teachers to display on screens during class
- to be shared with students when necessary (via URL + **password**)

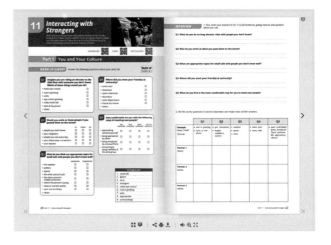

VOCABULARY LISTS

- Lists of key vocabulary are provided to help teachers efficiently cover the most challenging words and phrases on each page.

- If students need extra support, or if the teacher wants to expedite this step, Japanese translations are available through the **vocabulary** QR code on the first page of each unit (or through www.ibunka.jp).

  These pages are **protected by a password**, so teachers can decide whether or not to use them, depending on their personal preferences and their school's classroom language policies.

VOCABULARY
1. interactions
2. marital status
3. employment status
4. individual
5. in general terms
6. genre
7. with confidence
8. common ground
9. blend in
10. fade into the background
11. emphasize

ONLINE FORMS

These resources can be used:

- during class (to gather and display data from students) or
- as homework activities.

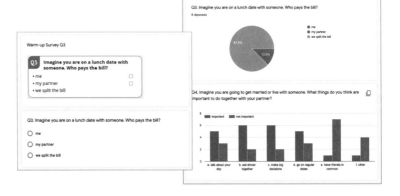

TEACHER'S MANUAL

The Teacher's Manual is available in both digital and print format. It contains:

- sample syllabi
- detailed advice on how to conduct classes in various contexts
- answers to all exercises
- authors' notes on each topic*

* Author's notes include a summary of each topic to provide teachers with some background information from intercultural research, and some commentary on the *Ibunka Survey* responses.

AUDIO TRACKS

All audio tracks can be downloaded, or played online. A set of three CDs is also available for purchase.

How to Access Teacher Resources

Teacher resources can be accessed through the QR codes on the first page of each unit, or the Ibunka website: www.ibunka.jp. They are **password-protected**. If you are using or have decided to use *Ibunka!* in your classes, please contact us to gain access to these resources.

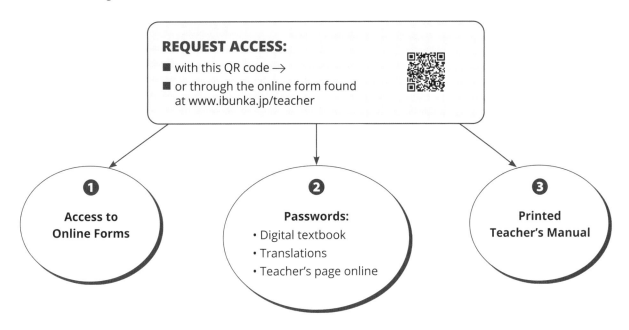

REQUEST ACCESS:
- with this QR code →
- or through the online form found at www.ibunka.jp/teacher

①
Access to Online Forms

②
Passwords:
- Digital textbook
- Translations
- Teacher's page online

③
Printed Teacher's Manual

Alma Publishing is a small, independent publishing company based in Kyoto. Founded by teachers, it is dedicated to developing teaching materials and teacher training centered on the realities of the Japanese classroom. Please don't hesitate to get in touch with us: contact@almalang.com.

And also...

MANGA CONTEST

- The *manga* activity is an optional way to let students be creative and end units on a fun note.
- If your students enjoy this activity, you could encourage them to enter their best work into our online *manga* contest each semester. You could even have the class vote on the best one for submission!

www.ibunka.jp/manga

IBUNKA SURVEY

- The survey this textbook is based on is an ongoing project. Students and teachers with international experience can contribute by filling out any of the eleven online forms.
- For more in-depth exchange of ideas on these intercultural topics, check out the online Ibunka Survey forum!

www.ibunka.jp/survey

1 *Introducing Yourself*

The ways in which we present ourselves are deeply cultural. When you introduce yourself, do you focus on your uniqueness, or on how much you have in common with others? And how do you respond to other people's self introductions? Do you usually compliment them?

VOCABULARY   AUDIO   FOR TEACHERS

Part 1 You and Your Culture

WARM-UP SURVEY *Answer the following questions about your daily life.*

WARM-UP SURVEY

Q1 Imagine you are going to introduce yourself to a group. What kinds of things would you mention about yourself?

- name ☐
- nickname ☐
- age ☐
- hometown ☐
- your favorite food ☐
- your school / job ☐
- family ☐
- a general hobby (e.g. games, music) ☐
- a specific hobby (e.g. chess, jazz) ☐
- your connection with the group ☐
- make a joke ☐
- other: ....

Q2 When describing your abilities to others, do you ...

- talk modestly, putting yourself down? ☐
- talk honestly? ☐
- talk yourself up? ☐

Q3 When you comment on what someone has said, do you compliment them (say positive things about them)?

- Yes, I always try to. ☐
- Only if I really feel that way. ☐
- No, I avoid complimenting. ☐

Q4 Do you think it's normal to comment on someone's appearance?

- Yes, in any case (positive or negative). ☐
- Yes, when it's positive (someone looks good). ☐
- No, never. It's rude. ☐

Q5 Imagine that you are introducing yourself at a club you just joined. What do you think you should do in order to make a good first impression?

- talk humbly about yourself ☐
- be well-dressed ☐
- make eye contact ☐
- use honorifics ☐
- smile ☐
- use humor ☐
- be well-groomed (hair, nails, makeup, etc.) ☐
- make jokes ☐
- laugh a lot ☐

VOCABULARY
1. to present oneself
2. uniqueness
3. to compliment
4. specific
5. modestly
6. to talk oneself up
7. to feel that way
8. appearance
9. to make a good first impression
10. honorifics
11. well-groomed

1. First, write your answers to Questions 1~5 in full sentences, giving reasons and opinions where you can.

Q1: What kinds of things do you mention when introducing yourself to a group?

....

....

Q2: How do you usually describe your abilities?

....

....

Q3: Do you usually compliment others?

....

....

Q4: Do you think it's normal to comment on someone's appearance?

....

....

Q5: What things should you do in order to make a good first impression?

....

....

2. Ask the survey questions to several classmates and make notes of their answers.

	Q1	Q2	Q3	Q4	Q5
Example Name: *Yurika*	• *name* • *nickname* • *hometown* • *age* • *general hobby*	• *talk modestly*	• *always tries to say positive things*	• *yes, but only when it's positive*	• *use honorifics (to show respect)* • *make eye contact*
Partner 1 Name:					
Partner 2 Name:					
Partner 3 Name:					

Now let's think about Japanese society and some differences between various groups. Write sentences using words and phrases from these lists.

meeting someone for the first time	
speaking to someone older	
speaking to someone younger	
taking a job interview	
introducing themselves to a class	
going on a first date	

1. I think that in Japan, when ⬚ ⬚ people tend to ⬚ .

2. In Japan, when speaking to someone you don't know well, it's common to ⬚ and to ⬚ .

3. ....
....
....

speak modestly
use humor
look for things in common
show confidence
use lots of *aizuchi*
give short responses
use honorifics
give compliments

How about you? Are you like most others in Japan, or do you have different views? Write more sentences about Japanese society, adding your own opinions or habits.

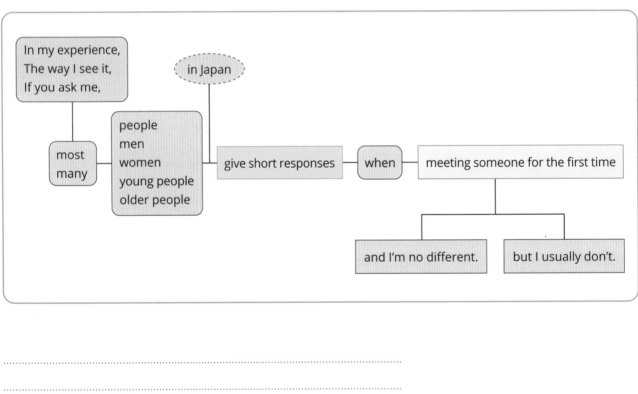

....
....
....
....
....
....
....

VOCABULARY
1. characteristics
2. modestly
3. things in common
4. in my experience, ...
5. if you ask me, ...
6. I'm no different.

People from a range of cultural backgrounds responded to the Ibunka Survey on this topic. Here are a few of their responses for you to read and think about. You will find more in the One Step Further section.

Q1 When you introduce yourself, do you focus on your uniqueness, or on how much you have in common with others? Have you noticed anything remarkable about the way people introduce themselves in the foreign cultures you have lived in?

Nira,
Costa Rican,
teacher,
lives in Japan

① In Japan, people seem to talk about their social situation (their employer or family) rather than about their private lives. I work for an English conversation school, so every month I have at least twenty "first-meeting" interactions with students. Very often after meeting someone for the first time, I feel that I know their marital and employment status but I don't know anything about them as individuals.

🔊 1-01

② When introducing myself in Japan, for example to other club members, I usually talked about my hobbies in very general terms, like "I like music" or "I like shopping". When I went to the US to study, I found myself saying much more detailed things, such as the genres of music I like. I got the feeling that most people wanted to be seen as unique. It was a bit stressful at first, but after some time I learned to talk about myself with confidence.

🔊 1-02

③ I think that experience has influenced how I talk about myself even now, after returning to Japan. But of course here I always start by looking for common ground.

🔊 1-03

Ryoji
Japanese,
software engineer,
has lived in the US

Émilie
French,
accountant,
lives in Japan

④ For me, It depends very much on my mood. When I'm in a good mood or a social mood, I try to draw attention to myself. I want to make an impression on the people I'm introducing myself to. But when I don't feel like talking, I try to blend in. I say only very general things, so that I'm not asked any questions. In France, this strategy works pretty well.

🔊 1-04

⑤ But in Japan, I have the impression that people are more interested in those who blend in. When I introduce myself by saying something very bland, they show their interest by asking questions. So I understand now that the strategies that helped me to "fade into the background" in France have the opposite effect here in Japan. And on the contrary, when I try to attract attention by emphasizing my uniqueness, I get very few questions in return. I never realized this difference before I took this survey!

🔊 1-05

COMPREHENSION 1

*Read the responses and mark the statements **true** or **false**.*

		True	False
①	Nira feels that she doesn't really know her clients personally after meeting them once.	☐	☐
②	In the US, Ryoji was upset that he could not find any music that he liked.	☐	☐
③	Over time, Ryoji changed his style of self-introduction.	☐	☐
④	In France, when Émilie doesn't want to talk, she gives very basic information about herself.	☐	☐
⑤	Emilie discovered that Japanese and French cultures have very similar styles of self-introduction.	☐	☐

VOCABULARY
1. interaction
2. marital status
3. employment status
4. in general terms
5. genre
6. with confidence
7. common ground
8. to blend in
9. bland
10. to fade into the background
11. to emphasize ~

Q2 Do you think you are usually modest when talking about yourself, or do you prefer to describe yourself in a positive light? How about people in foreign countries you have lived in?

6 Having been raised in England, I tend to _____ any strengths I might have. I think this is a cultural trait. In British culture, one cannot appear to _____. If I say I am not clever, or not good at something, then I can take it off the table as a topic and no one can _____ me or _____ fun of me.

🔊 1-06

Catriona
British,
writer,
lives in Japan

boast
make
criticize
downplay

7 I don't _____ to talk about my abilities to a Westerner I have just met, but I avoid doing it when speaking with Japanese people. I guess that's because it can be interpreted as arrogance, and _____ both professional and friendly relationships.

🔊 1-07

Jane
New Zealander,
teacher,
lives in Japan

stand out
describe
hesitate
harm

8 In my work as a teacher, I have noticed that some of my Japanese students tend to _____ themselves as "incompetent" and to choose a level that is too low for their actual abilities. One of my students, who is very bright, sometimes makes mistakes on purpose so as not to _____ from the group.

🔊 1-08

DISCUSSION

Which one of the survey responses on pages 11 and 12 was most interesting to you? Explain your choice, using the patterns below as a starting point. Then discuss it with classmates.

I found **A** Nira 's response to be the most **B** interesting . **C** Personally, I tend to ...

A	
1	Nira
2	Ryori
3	Émilie
4	Catriona
5	Jane

B	
1	interesting
2	relatable
3	peculiar
4	striking

C	
1	Personally, I tend to ...
2	It seems that ...
3	I find it surprising that ...
4	I always thought that ...

VOCABULARY
1. to downplay ~
2. cultural trait
3. to take ~ off the table
4. to be interpreted as ~
5. arrogance
6. incompetent
7. on purpose
8. to stand out
9. relatable
10. peculiar
11. striking
12. to tend to ~

Q3 **Do you usually compliment people? How do you respond to compliments?**

Marc
Belgian,
businessman,
lives in Japan

⑨ I compliment people if I really mean it. In the same vein, I don't like to be complimented when I know it's not justified. I feel embarrassed. I've noticed that Japanese people compliment each other consistently. It seems to me that it's a social rule. It "puts oil on the wheels" and makes for harmonious relationships. But personally I prefer more spontaneous, honest communication.

🔊 **1-09**

Joe
American,
university professor,
lives in Japan,
has lived in France

⑩ I tend to give lots of compliments when I speak Japanese. In the US, I give some compliments. In France, very few - it seems less common.

🔊 **1-10**

Masako
Japanese,
salesperson,
has lived in Canada

⑪ What surprised me at first when I came into contact with people from Canada was that, unlike in Japan, they openly praise their own family and relatives and accept compliments. When I first started interacting with others, I felt it was tiresome because I couldn't take praise honestly, and had trouble reacting to it.

🔊 **1-11**

		True	False
⑨	Marc thinks that it is best to always compliment people in another culture, regardless of how you feel.	☐	☐
⑩	Joe is certainly more likely to compliment others in Japan than in his home culture.	☐	☐
⑪	In Canada, Masako found it difficult to think of compliments for people she met.	☐	☐

CREATIVITY | *Draw a simple manga based on the topic of this unit. It may be from your experience or your imagination.*

1	2

3	4

VOCABULARY
1. in the same vein
2. not justified
3. harmonious
4. regardless of ~
5. openly
6. to praise ~
7. praise
8. tiresome

2 Sleep and Rest

Attitudes to sleep and tiredness are quite varied across cultures. How long, where, when and with whom do we sleep? How important is it to "manage your sleep"?

VOCABULARY   AUDIO   FOR TEACHERS

Part 1   You and Your Culture

WARM-UP SURVEY   *Answer the following questions about your daily life.*

WARM-UP SURVEY

Q1 On average, how many hours a night do you sleep?

5 or less ☐	8 ☐
6 ☐	9 or more ☐
7 ☐	

Is that enough for you? Yes ☐ No ☐

Q2 Do you ever sleep during the daytime? Where?

	always	often	some-times	never
• in my room	☐	☐	☐	☐
• on the train or bus	☐	☐	☐	☐
• in class	☐	☐	☐	☐
• during break times	☐	☐	☐	☐
• other:	☐	☐	☐	☐

Q3 Do you think that it's OK to sleep in these situations?

	OK	not OK
• in a class of less than 20 people	☐	☐
• in a class of more than 50 people	☐	☐
• on campus, between classes	☐	☐
• on the train or bus	☐	☐
• in a library	☐	☐
• at a *hanami* party	☐	☐
• during a long meeting	☐	☐
• other:	☐	☐

Q4 What kinds of things prevent you from getting a good night's sleep?

• work	☐
• study	☐
• noise	☐
• people around me	☐
• distractions (TV, internet, etc.)	☐
• other	☐

Q5 Do you think it's important to manage your sleep- i.e., to get a decent amount of sleep, and to maintain a regular bedtime and wake-up time?

• Yes, because I want to ...
  - stay in good health.   ☐
  - have enough energy.   ☐
  - be sharp for my studies.   ☐
  - work efficiently.   ☐
  - look and feel my best.   ☐

• I want to, but in fact ...
  - I have too much study (work).   ☐
  - distractions (e.g. smartphone, TV) take away my sleep time.   ☐
  - I don't have a regular bedtime.   ☐

• No, it's not especially important to me.   ☐

VOCABULARY

1. break times
2. on campus
3. a good night's sleep
4. distractions
5. decent
6. to maintain ~
7. to be sharp
8. efficiently
9. to look one's best
10. to feel one's best

First, write your answers to Questions 1~5 in full sentences, giving reasons and opinions where you can.

Q1: On average, how many hours a day do you sleep? Is that enough for you?

....

....

Q2: Do you ever sleep during the daytime? If so, where?

....

....

Q3: In what situations do you think it's OK to sleep during the day?

....

....

Q4: What kinds of things prevent you from getting a good night's sleep?

....

....

Q5: Do you think it's important to manage your sleep?

....

....

2. Ask the survey questions to several classmates and make notes of their answers.

	Q1	Q2	Q3	Q4	Q5
Example Name: *Sara*	• about 6 hours • not enough for her	• often naps in her room • sometimes on the train	• in a class of more than 50 people • on the train	• study • noise (traffic) • smartphone	• yes, but she has too much study
Partner 1 Name:					
Partner 2 Name:					
Partner 3 Name:					

Now let's think about Japanese society and some differences between various groups. Write sentences using words and phrases from these lists.

| university students |
| office workers |
| convenience store workers |
| construction workers |
| the elderly |
| students who play sport |
| students who attend *juku* |
| commuters |
| |

1. In my opinion, ⬚
in Japan tend to ⬚.

2. I think that ⬚
are more likely than ⬚
⬚ to ⬚
⬚.

3. ....
....
....

| get a good night's sleep |
| sleep in public |
| stay up all night |
| suffer from lack of sleep |
| take power naps |
| sleep in class |
| sleep whenever they can |
| nod off during the day |
| |

How about you? Are you like most others in Japan, or do you have different views? Write more sentences about Japanese society, adding your own opinions or habits.

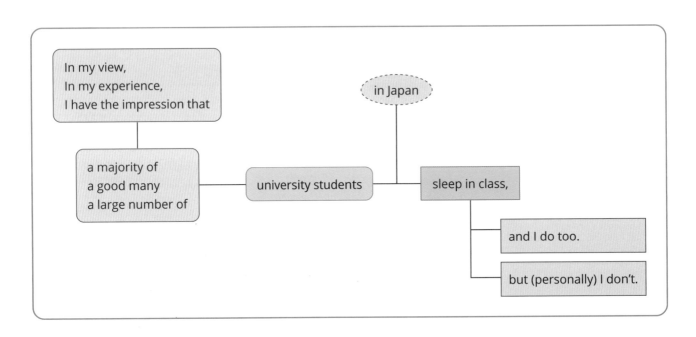

In my view,
In my experience,
I have the impression that

a majority of
a good many
a large number of

university students

in Japan

sleep in class,

and I do too.

but (personally) I don't.

....
....
....
....
....
....
....

VOCABULARY
1. construction workers
2. commuters
3. to stay up all night
4. power nap
5. to nod off
6. in my view ~
7. I have the impression that ~
8. a majority of ~
9. a good many ~

People from a range of cultural backgrounds responded to the Ibunka Survey on this topic. Here are a few of their responses for you to read and think about. You will find more in the One Step Further section.

Q1   **What are your thoughts on how people sleep or deal with tiredness in foreign countries where you have lived?**

Matt
American,
publisher,
has lived in Japan

❶ When I lived in Japan, it seemed most people were overly tired; deprived of free time and sleep time. It was interesting to watch people doze off on the train and then suddenly, as if by magic, wake up just as they arrived at their station. How did they do that?

🔊 **2-01**

❷ There also seemed to be a kind of perverse pride taken in doing an "all-nighter." I thought it was strange that people would stay up all night to work or study, as if they were showing commitment, and proving they were tough enough to fight off sleep in order to work or study more.

🔊 **2-02**

❸ I believe most Japanese people don't get enough sleep. You can see people sleeping in public spaces like buses and trains, and even in business meetings or conferences. I guess that in the Japanese workplace, being productive and efficient is not as important as just showing up.

Miki
Japanese,
writer,
has lived in the UK

🔊 **2-03**

COMPREHENSION 1   *Read the responses and mark the statements true or false.*

		True	False
❶	Matt was surprised at the sleeping habits of people on trains in Japan.	☐	☐
❷	Matt thinks that staying up all night is the best way to show that you are a hard worker.	☐	☐
❸	According to Miki, efficiency takes top priority in workplaces in Japan.	☐	☐

VOCABULARY
1. overly
2. deprived of ~
3. as if by magic
4. perverse
5. to do an "all-nighter"
6. commitment
7. productive
8. to show up
9. to take top priority

COMPREHENSION 2 — Read the responses and fill in the gaps with the correct words.

Q2 In the countries you have lived in, would you say that it's considered important to get enough sleep and maintain a regular bedtime?

Stéphane
French,
architect,
lives in Japan

④ It is indeed. When I was a child, my parents had a strict rule _____ the week that we had to go to bed at 9 p.m. This rule continued _____ I was about 13 or 14 years old. _____ we got up _____ 7 a.m., this ensured us about 9 or 10 hours of sleep. There were no naps, so we had to get a good night's sleep.

🔊 2-04

> during
> around
> since
> until

Motoko
Japanese,
homemaker,
has lived
in Australia

⑤ I was surprised at how strictly Australian parents _____ their children's bedtime and _____ them to bed quite early. There was even a cute character (a person dressed in an animal suit) that would _____ on TV screens at 7:30 in the evening and tell all children under the age of 12 to _____. We don't have anything like that in Japan.

🔊 2-05

> appear
> control
> go to bed
> send

DISCUSSION

Which one of the survey responses on pages 17 and 18 was most interesting to you? Explain your choice, using the patterns below as a starting point. Then discuss it with classmates.

I found [A] Miki 's response to be the most [B] relatable. [C] Personally, I tend to ...

A	
1	Matt
2	Miki
3	Stéphane
4	Motoko

B	
1	interesting
2	relatable
3	strange
4	thought-provoking

C	
1	Personally, I tend to ...
2	It seems that ...
3	I find it surprising that ...
4	I always thought that ...

....
....
....
....
....
....
....
....

VOCABULARY
1. indeed
2. to ensure ~
3. nap
4. strictly
5. animal suit
6. strange
7. thought-provoking

*Read the responses and mark the statements **true** or **false**.*

Takako
Japanese,
company employee,
has lived in Belgium
and France

6 I did a year of study abroad at a university in Belgium. It was pretty tough because I had to work hard at my French to be able to keep up with the rest of the class. I often stayed up late studying, so sometimes I would fall asleep in class. One day, one of my teachers got really upset with me and woke me up. He said, "If you're coming here to sleep, you might as well stay at home!"

🔊 2-07

7 I'm an engineer, and I was posted to the Tokyo branch of my company for three years. From time to time we had to make presentations to potential clients. The day before, I always made a point of going home early, in order to get a good night's sleep and be as sharp as I could on the big day. But my Japanese colleagues always stayed extra late on those occasions. That always shocked me, but I'm pretty sure they felt the same way about me.

Jurgen
German,
engineer,
has lived in Japan

🔊 2-08

	True	False
6 Takako got upset at her teachers in Belgium because they didn't let her sleep in class.	☐	☐
7 Jurgen thinks that on the night before an important task, it's better to get enough rest than to work late.	☐	☐

CREATIVITY *Draw a simple* manga *based on the topic of this unit. It may be from your experience or your imagination.*

1	**2**

3	**4**

VOCABULARY
1. tough
2. to keep up with ~
3. to stay up
4. upset
5. to be posted to ~
6. from time to time
7. potential clients
8. to make a point of ~
9. sharp
10. the big day
11. extra late

3 In the Classroom

If you have ever studied abroad, you may have noticed that classroom behavior is quite different from culture to culture. In your country, are classes usually interactive? Do students actively ask and answer questions, or are they usually silent? Who is doing most of the talking in the classroom?

VOCABULARY   AUDIO   FOR TEACHERS

Part 1 You and Your Culture

WARM-UP SURVEY *Please answer the following questions about your daily life.*

WARM-UP
SURVEY

Q1 If your teacher asks a question to the whole class, do you raise your hand to answer?

- always ☐
- most of the time ☐
- sometimes ☐
- almost never ☐
- never ☐

Q2 When do you find it easiest to speak up in class? → *choose two*

- When the teacher is friendly. ☐
- When the number of students is small. ☐
- When I know most of my classmates. ☐
- When I have something to contribute. ☐
- When I am interested in the topic. ☐
- Other: ....

Q3 Which learning style do you enjoy most?

- Lecture style: teacher talks and students take notes ☐
- Discussion style: teacher guides students through class discussion ☐
- Project style: teacher assigns a task, and students work together in small groups ☐

Q4 If the teacher asks you a question in class and you don't know the answer, what do you usually do? → *choose two*

- I wait in silence for the teacher to ask someone else. ☐
- I say, "I don't know" straight away. ☐
- I look in the textbook for the answer. ☐
- I ask my neighbor for help. ☐
- I quickly guess at an answer. ☐
- I think carefully before making a guess. ☐
- Other: ....

Q5 Why do you think some students usually remain silent after being asked a question by the teacher in class ? → *choose two*

- They don't have confidence in their answer. ☐
- They don't know the answer. ☐
- They don't want to make a mistake. ☐
- They don't want to hold up the class. ☐
- They don't want to look stupid. ☐
- They don't want to appear to show off. ☐
- They know that the teacher will ask someone else. ☐

VOCABULARY
1. interactive
2. most of the time
3. to speak up
4. learning style
5. lecture
6. to assign ~
7. straight away
8. to remain silent
9. to hold up (the class)
10. to show off

1. First, write your answers to Questions 1~5 in full sentences, giving reasons and opinions where you can.

Q1: When your teacher asks a question to the whole class, do you usually raise your hand?

....

....

Q2: When do you find it easiest to speak up in class?

....

....

Q3: What kind of learning style do you enjoy most? Why?

....

....

Q4: If the teacher asks you a question in class and you don't know the answer, what do you usually do?

....

....

Q5: Why do you think students usually remain silent after being asked a question by the teacher?

....

....

2. Ask the survey questions to three classmates and make notes of their answers.

	Q1	Q2	Q3	Q4	Q5
Example Name: *Akira*	• almost never	• when he knows his classmates • when the teacher is friendly	• discussion style (more fun)	• looks in his textbook • asks neighbors for help	• most students don't want to look stupid • they know the teacher will ask someone else
Partner 1 Name:					
Partner 2 Name:					
Partner 3 Name:					

EXPRESSION 1

Now let's think about Japanese society and some differences between various groups. Write sentences using words and phrases from these lists.

shy students	
confident students	
students in co-ed schools	
students in girls' schools	
students in boys' schools	
returnees	
boys	
girls	

1. In Japan, I think there is a tendency for ____ ____ to ____ ____ in class.

2. I feel that in classrooms in Japan, ____ ____ ____ more than ____ do.

3. ....
....

remain silent
guess at answers
ask questions
avoid speaking
pretend to understand
pretend not to understand
take risks
prefer to study alone
prefer to study in pairs

EXPRESSION 2

How about you? Are you like most others in Japan, or do you have different views? Write more sentences about Japanese society, adding your own opinions or habits.

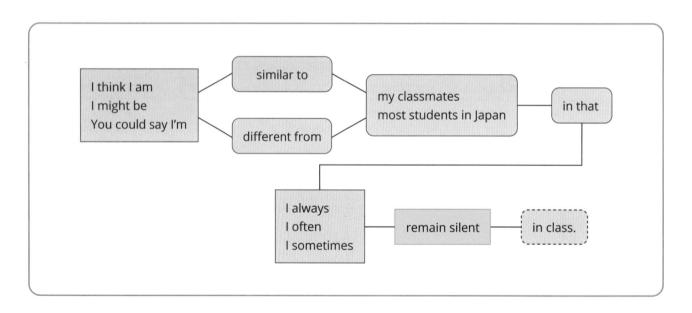

....
....
....
....
....
....
....

VOCABULARY
1. there is a tendency for ~ to ~
2. co-ed school
3. returnee
4. to guess at ~
5. to avoid
6. to pretend to (not to) ~
7. in pairs
8. I might be ~
9. You could say I'm ~
10. in that ~

Part 2 People in Other Cultures

People from a range of cultural backgrounds responded to the Ibunka Survey on this topic. Here are a few of their responses for you to read and think about. You will find more in the One Step Further section.

Q1 In the country you grew up in, are classes usually interactive? For example, when a teacher asks a question to the whole class, do students volunteer to reply? Do they freely ask questions to the teacher?

Q2 Do students ever remain silent even after having been asked a question by the teacher?

Jeremy
American, university professor, lives in Japan

1 In my American high school, sometimes when the teacher asked a question that was too hard or too easy, students hesitated to raise their hands. But overall, much of the class was a dialogue between the teacher and individual students who raised their hands, and sometimes even disagreed with the teacher.

🔊 **3-01**

2 Being able to give an opinion was an important part of understanding the material. If the teacher asked a question and no one raised their hand, it seemed rather unfriendly.

🔊 **3-02**

Hayley
Australian, study abroad advisor, lives in the UK

3 Growing up in Australia, classes were always interactive. Students were encouraged to contribute throughout the lesson. I could freely ask my teacher for more information if I needed it.

🔊 **3-03**

4 Also, students almost always answered when called upon by the teacher. It was very rare for a student to remain silent. If they did, it was usually because they were extremely shy. At that point, the teacher would ask other students to help the student out, and the lesson would move on.

🔊 **3-04**

COMPREHENSION 1 Read the responses and mark the statements **true** or **false**.

		True	False
1	In Jeremy's high school, it was common for students to have conversations with the teacher during class.	☐	☐
2	Jeremy felt that students who disagreed with their teacher were quite rude.	☐	☐
3	Hayley was too shy to ever ask her teacher for help.	☐	☐
4	In Hayley's experience, classes did not progress if a student didn't answer the teacher's question.	☐	☐

VOCABULARY
1. to volunteer to ~
2. to hesitate to ~
3. overall
4. material
5. to contribute
6. throughout ~
7. to be called upon
8. to help out
9. to move on

Read the responses and fill in the gaps with the correct words.

5
I cannot say that classes in France are interactive, at least not in my _____. Most of my teachers did a lot of the talking and students just listened and took _____.

🔊 3-05

Thierry,
French,
company employee,
lives in Canada

6
But students are expected to respond when a teacher asks them a question. If there is _____, it's very short. The student might say something like, "I don't know," or, "I forgot." The teacher would then move on to another student. French teachers and students are generally uncomfortable with silence. It feels odd if there is no _____ from the student. This may upset the teacher, and they will usually show it.

🔊 3-06

reply
silence
experience
notes

DISCUSSION

Which one of the survey responses on pages 23 and 24 was most interesting to you? Explain your choice, using the patterns below as a starting point. Then discuss it with classmates.

I found [A] Jeremy 's response to be the most [B] surprising . [C] I didn't realize that ...

A	
1	Jeremy
2	Hayley
3	Thierry

B	
1	interesting
2	surprising
3	relatable
4	shocking

C	
1	I didn't realize that ...
2	I had always thought that ...
3	In my experience ...
4	As for me, I ...

VOCABULARY
1. to be expected to ~
2. to respond
3. uncomfortable
4. odd
5. upset
6. to find ~ to be ~
7. relatable
8. I didn't realize that ...
9. I had always thought that ...

CULTURE SHOCK

Two people – a teacher and a student – responded to the Ibunka Survey *talking about their different views on the same topic. Read the responses and mark the statements* **true** *or* **false**.

Carmen
Spanish,
teacher,
lives in Japan

7 In Japan, I was faced many times with a difficult situation: a student staying completely silent after I asked them a question in front of the whole class. As a language teacher, that was hard to take. I felt a lot of pressure when it happened to me but I tried to hide it, to show I was in control of the class. I don't think my students knew I was feeling so stressed.

🔊 3-07

9 I did a one-year study abroad program in the US. The biggest shock I had in class was about how quickly everyone was replying. I remember being surprised when a classmate was put on the spot by the teacher and said, "I'm not sure" without blinking an eye. I wondered why he wasn't looking a bit harder for the answer. But everyone seemed to be OK with that.

🔊 3-09

8 In Spain, a student not responding to a direct question would mean that the student is defying the teacher's authority. It's quite embarrassing for everyone.

🔊 3-08

10 Gradually I got into the habit of replying straight away whenever I was asked a question, even if I didn't know the answer.

🔊 3-10

Ken
Japanese,
employee,
has lived in the US

		True	False
7	Carmen sometimes felt stress and pressure in Japanese classrooms because students didn't respond to her questions.	☐	☐
8	In the culture Carmen grew up in, it's considered rude for students to say, "I don't know" directly to their teacher.	☐	☐
9	Ken was surprised at how hard American students looked for the answers to their teacher's questions.	☐	☐
10	After some time, Ken became able to respond to his teacher within a few seconds.	☐	☐

CREATIVITY

Draw a simple manga *based on the topic of this unit. It may be from your experience or your imagination.*

1	2

3	4

VOCABULARY
1. to be faced with ~
2. hard to take
3. in control of ~
4. a direct question
5. to defy
6. authority
7. to be put on the spot
8. without blinking an eye
9. gradually
10. rude
11. to look hard for ~
12. within a few seconds

4 Having Guests in Your Home

When you spend time with others, is it in your home, or in public places such as restaurants? And when you are invited to someone's place, are you given a tour and told to "help yourself"... or not?

VOCABULARY   AUDIO   FOR TEACHERS

Part 1 You and Your Culture

WARM-UP SURVEY *Answer the following questions about your daily life.*

WARM-UP SURVEY

Q1 Who do you currently live with?

- my parent(s) ☐
- my brother(s) / sister(s) ☐
- my spouse / partner ☐
- my girlfriend / boyfriend ☐
- my child / children ☐
- my grandfather / my grandmother ☐
- I live by myself. ☐
- other: ....

Q2 How often do people come to your home?

	a few times a week	a few times a month	once a month or so	once or twice a year	almost never	never
relatives*	☐	☐	☐	☐	☐	☐
friends*	☐	☐	☐	☐	☐	☐
colleagues / classmates	☐	☐	☐	☐	☐	☐
neighbors	☐	☐	☐	☐	☐	☐
other:						

*or the relatives / friends of my spouse / partner

Q3 What do people visit your house for?

	just to drop by	just to hang out	to have drinks	for a meal	to stay over
relatives*	☐	☐	☐	☐	☐
friends*	☐	☐	☐	☐	☐
colleagues	☐	☐	☐	☐	☐
neighbors	☐	☐	☐	☐	☐
other:					

*or the relatives / friends of my spouse / partner

Q4 Which rooms in your house do you let guests (aside from relatives) into?

- I live in a one-room apartment. ☐
- entry hall ☐
- guest reception room ☐
- living room ☐
- kitchen ☐
- my bedroom ☐
- parents' bedroom ☐
- bathroom ☐

Do you give a tour of your house to guests (aside from relatives)?

- Yes ☐
- No ☐

Q5 Do you prefer to spend time with people in private homes, or in public places such as cafes? Why?

- Private homes, because ...
  - it's more relaxing. ☐
  - it's more intimate. ☐
  - it's cheaper. ☐
  - it's more fun. ☐
- Public places (like cafes or restaurants), because ...
  - it's more convenient. ☐
  - I want some privacy. ☐
  - I don't want to cook. ☐
  - it's a hassle to tidy up. ☐
  - I don't want people to see my things. ☐
  - my house is a mess. ☐

VOCABULARY	
1. to give a tour	7. to let guests into ~
2. to help yourself	8. relatives
3. currently	9. entry hall
4. by myself	10. intimate
5. to drop by	11. hassle
6. to stay over	12. to tidy up

1. First, write your answers to Questions 1~5 in full sentences, giving reasons and opinions where you can.

Q1: Who do you currently live with?

....

....

Q2: How often do people come to your home?

....

....

Q3: What do people visit your house for?

....

....

Q4: Which rooms in your house do you let guests into? Do you give them a tour of your house?

....

....

Q5: Do you prefer to spend time with people in private homes, or in public places such as cafes? Why?

....

....

2. Ask the survey questions to three classmates and make notes of their answers.

	Q1	Q2	Q3	Q4	Q5
Example Name: *Jun*	• *with his parents*	• *relatives: once a month* • *friends: sometimes* • *neighbors: once a year*	• *relatives: meal / stay over* • *friends: drinks / meal* • *neighbors: drop by*	• *friends: living room, my bedroom* • *neighbors: entry hall* • *Tour? Never!*	• *prefers cafes in general* • *sometimes invites friends when his parents are not home*
Partner 1 Name:					
Partner 2 Name:					
Partner 3 Name:					

Now let's think about Japanese society and some differences between various groups. Write sentences using words and phrases from these lists.

| university students |
| homemakers |
| salaried workers |
| elderly people |
| people living alone |
| couples with young children |
| |
| |
| |

1. I think that in Japan, ☐

☐ prefer to ☐

☐ rather than

☐.

2. In my opinion, ☐

are more likely than ☐

☐ to invite people into their home.

3. ....

....

| socialize in restaurants |
| go for after-work drinks |
| eat out with friends |
| invite people over |
| host parties at home |
| socialize outdoors |
| meet people in cafes |
| |
| |

How about you? Are you like most others in Japan, or do you have different views? Write more sentences about Japanese society, adding your own opinions or habits.

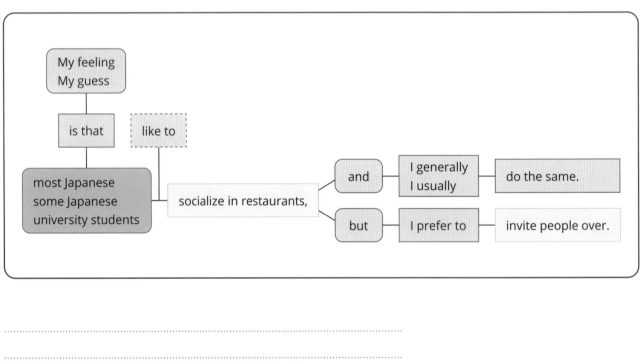

....

....

....

....

....

....

....

VOCABULARY
1. homemakers
2. to invite people over
3. to socialize
4. to host ~
5. outdoors
6. My guess is that ...
7. generally

People from a range of cultural backgrounds responded to the Ibunka Survey on this topic. Here are a few of their responses for you to read and think about. You will find more in the One Step Further section.

Q1 In the culture you grew up in, is it common to invite people into one's home to socialize? How about in other cultures you have experienced?

❶ Yes. It is very common. In fact, when I was growing up, it wasn't uncommon for my friends to be over at my parents' house, even when I wasn't there! I sometimes returned home from my part-time job to find friends in my basement playing video games with my brothers.

🔊 **4-01**

Billy
Canadian,
accounts manager,
lives in Japan

❷ I am American and I have a fairly open attitude towards socializing at home. I enjoy inviting people over casually, for a drink or coffee, for example. But for my Japanese wife, there is no such thing as a "casual" visit from a guest. For her, the house is reserved almost exclusively for visits from family.

🔊 **4-02**

Bob
American,
professor,
lives in Japan

❸ I don't mind meeting people at restaurants, but all my friends have come to my place and had dinner together many times. I can open up and show my true self that way. If someone had never visited my home, I would feel strange about calling that person a friend.

🔊 **4-03**

Maya
Spanish,
photographer,
has lived in the UK

COMPREHENSION 1　Read the responses and mark the statements **true** or **false**.

	True	False
❶ In the culture Billy grew up in, most people don't usually socialize in their homes.	☐	☐
❷ Bob and his wife have very similar views about inviting people to their house.	☐	☐
❸ Maya believes that showing someone your living space is an important part of friendship.	☐	☐

VOCABULARY
1. not uncommon for ~ to ~
2. basement
3. fairly
4. attitude
5. no such thing as ~
6. reserved for ~
7. exclusively
8. to open up
9. living space

Q2 **Do you usually give a tour of your home to guests?**

4

Sure, I do. I want them to be able to really _____. Once I've shown them around most of the rooms and where everything is, my guests are free to _____ themselves to any food or drink, and then they don't _____ me to guide them. In this way, they can truly _____ at home.

Jeremy
American,
cook,
has lived in Italy

help
relax
feel
need

🔊 4-04

5

No. When I was a teenager I used to _____ friends to my bedroom so we could chat in private. But now that I'm an adult and I _____ my own place, nobody comes to my bedroom. I would never _____ of showing that space to people now, even my close friends. We just _____ in the living room or the kitchen.

Isabelle
French,
consultant,
has lived in the US

hang out
think
have
bring

🔊 4-05

DISCUSSION *Which one of the survey responses on pages 29 and 30 was most interesting to you? Explain your choice, using the vocabulary in the box below. Then discuss your choice with classmates.*

I found **A** Billy 's response to be the most **B** intriguing . **C** I never imagined that …

A	
1	Billy
2	Bob
3	Maya
4	Jeremy
5	Isabelle

B	
1	interesting
2	surprising
3	understandable
4	intriguing

C	
1	I never imagined that …
2	In my experience, …
3	As for me, …
4	I didn't know that …

....
....
....
....
....
....
....

VOCABULARY
1. to show ~ around
2. where everything is
3. my own place
4. to hang out
5. understandable
6. intriguing

*Read the responses and mark the statements **true** or **false**.*

> **Q3** **Have you ever experienced a communication gap or misunderstanding in a foreign culture, with regard to having guests in the home?**

Dave
Canadian,
English teacher,
lives in Japan

❻ *I've been married to my Japanese wife Yukiko for five years. She always says "Go out with your friends," but I'd like her to meet them too! Back home in Canada, my parents often invited couples over for dinner, and they would bring their kids with them too. In that sense, it's a little lonely. I feel like we're leading disconnected lives.*

🔊 4-06

❼ *Four years ago I did a homestay in Perth, Australia. My host mother was a charming lady. She showed me all over the house, and told me to help myself to any food to make my own breakfasts and lunches. At first, I was too shy to even open the fridge by myself, and barely ate anything the first week! I can laugh about it now, because now I see that hosts and guests sometimes have very different expectations.*

Manami
Japanese,
sales staff,
has lived in Australia

🔊 4-07

	True	False
❻ Dave feels disappointed that he and his wife don't socialize together.		☐
❼ Manami found it easy to freely take food from her host mother's fridge.		☐

Draw a simple manga based on the topic of this unit. It may be from your experience or your imagination.

1	2

3	4

VOCABULARY
1. in that sense
2. to lead a ~ life
3. disconnected
4. charming
5. barely

5 In the Clubhouse

Belonging to a club while at school has a huge influence on the way we learn to behave as members of society. But how much time and effort should you put into it? What we feel is "normal" or "appropriate" is quite different across cultures.

VOCABULARY   AUDIO   FOR TEACHERS

Part 1 You and Your Culture

WARM-UP SURVEY *Answer the following questions about your daily life.*

Q1 Have you ever been a member of a school club or circle? Which ones?

	club	circle	neither
• in university	☐	☐	☐
• in high school	☐	☐	☐
• in junior high school	☐	☐	☐
• in elementary school	☐	☐	☐

Q2 If you were in a club in high school, what was your main reason for joining it?

- interest ☐
- my ability / skill ☐
- parents' influence ☐
- wanting to stay active ☐
- wanting to make friends ☐
- the relatively light commitment ☐
- friendly clubmates ☐
- to help get into university ☐
- other: ....

If you were <u>not</u> in a club in high school, what was your main reason for not joining one?

- lack of interest ☐
- lack of skills ☐
- lack of self-confidence ☐
- lack of time (busy with studies) ☐
- lack of time (long commute) ☐
- it wasn't common / popular ☐
- other: ....

Q3 What do you think are the benefits of being in a school club? → *choose three*

- friendships ☐
- gaining self-confidence ☐
- improving skills ☐
- learning teamwork ☐
- gaining social experience ☐
- gaining self-discipline ☐
- gaining mental toughness ☐
- the sense of achievement ☐
- staying healthy and active ☐
- other: ....

Q4 Do you think that doing club activities five times a week at university is worth the time and effort?

- Yes, definitely. Once you have joined a club it's your duty to give it your best effort. ☐
- Yes, probably. As a team member it's your duty to support your teammates. ☐
- Not really. Studying should be a student's first duty. ☐
- No, that is just too much time to put in. ☐

Q5 What do you think is the ideal frequency for club activities at university?

- Once or twice a week. ☐
- Three or four times a week. ☐
- Five or more times a week. ☐
- Only when it is necessary. ☐

VOCABULARY

1. influence	7. self-discipline
2. to stay active	8. mental toughness
3. relatively	9. sense of achievement
4. light commitment	10. duty
5. self-confidence	11. frequency
6. commute	12. only when it is necessary

1. First, write your answers to Questions 1~5 in full sentences, giving reasons and opinions where you can.

Q1: Have you ever been a member of a school club or circle?

....

....

Q2: What were the reasons you joined (didn't join) a club in high school?

....

....

Q3: What do you think are the benefits of being in a school club?

....

....

Q4: Do you think that doing club activities five times a week at university is worth the time and effort?

....

....

Q5: What do you think is the ideal frequency for club activities at university?

....

....

2. Ask the survey questions to three classmates and make notes of their answers.

	Q1	Q2	Q3	Q4	Q5
Example Name: *Naomi*	• volleyball club in HS • volunteer circle at uni	• wanted to make friends	• friendship • learning teamwork	• no, that's to much time to put in	• once or twice a week is enough
Partner 1 Name:					
Partner 2 Name:					
Partner 3 Name:					

Now let's think about Japanese society and some differences between various groups. Write sentences using words and phrases from these lists.

sports clubs		long hours
art clubs		heavy commitments
music groups		relaxed schedules
famous clubs		strict rules
volunteer circles		strict hierarchies
clubs at private schools		close bonds
clubs at public schools		opportunities to learn
clubs in high school		skilled instructors
clubs at universities		

1. I think that in Japan, _____ _____ generally have _____.

2. I would say that _____ are more common in _____ than they are in _____.

3. ....
....

How about you? Are you like most others in Japan, or do you have different views? Write more sentences about Japanese society, adding your own opinions or habits.

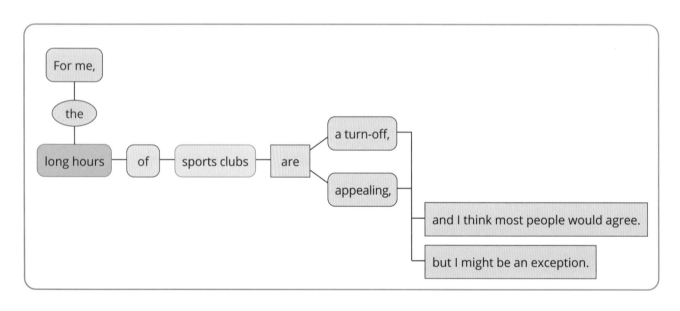

For me, the long hours of sports clubs are a turn-off, / appealing, and I think most people would agree. / but I might be an exception.

VOCABULARY
1. private school
2. public school
3. long hours
4. heavy commitments
5. relaxed schedules
6. strict rules
7. strict hierarchies
8. close bonds
9. a turn-off
10. appealing
11. an exception

Part 2　People in Other Cultures

People from a range of cultural backgrounds responded to the Ibunka Survey on this topic. Here are a few of their responses for you to read and think about. You will find more in the One Step Further section.

Q1 Were you in any clubs (sports, music, other activities) during your school years? If you were how much time did you spend on clubs per week? Is that typical of the culture you grew up in?

Q2 Do you have any experiences related to clubs in the foreign country you are living in or have lived in?

Sam
Australian,
artistic director,
has lived in the UK

❶ When I was in primary school, my brothers and I played tennis in a local club. It was a lot of fun. We practiced once a week after school, and had matches at other local clubs on Saturday mornings.

🔊 **5-01**

❷ Looking back, I feel it was just the right amount of time to invest in it. I'm glad I did it- it was the perfect diversion from my studies, and it kept me outdoors and active.

🔊 **5-02**

❸ In my opinion, there is no real "school club" culture in France. In my case, I never belonged to a club when I was at school. I only attended art classes on Wednesdays, and dance classes on Saturdays- both separately from school. There were no clubs at university either.

🔊 **5-03**

Stéphanie
French,
teacher,
lives in Japan

❹ It took me a long time to realize what my students meant when they talked about gasshuku. In France, very few people join clubs at school. So the idea of going somewhere and staying overnight with other club members was almost impossible for me to imagine.

🔊 **5-04**

COMPREHENSION 1　Read the responses and mark the statements **true** or **false**.

		True	False
❶	Sam spent at least four days a week at his tennis club when he was at primary school.	☐	☐
❷	Sam thought his tennis club took too much time from his studies.	☐	☐
❸	Stéphanie went to two cultural clubs at her high school: art and dance.	☐	☐
❹	In France, staying somewhere overnight with clubmates is an extremely rare thing.	☐	☐

VOCABULARY
1.　primary school
2.　to invest time in ~
3.　diversion
4.　no real ~
5.　the idea of ~

Catriona
British,
writer,
lives in Japan

⑤
In Japan, three of my children were in clubs. One daughter was in the softball club in junior and senior high school. She had overwhelmingly _____ experiences, which I believe impact her life today. However, right from the outset it was _____ that there would be no time for anything else, and no family time. She had _____ morning practice, so she left before 6 a.m. She also had evening practice every day, and matches all day every weekend. At New Year, Obon and around test time she sometimes got a few _____ days off.

clear
early
precious
positive

🔊 5-05

Junya
Japanese,
barista,
has lived in Nepal

⑥
I belonged to the soccer club from when I was in elementary school, all the _____ through to the end of high school. It did take a lot of my time and _____ , but I feel that my club activities made me a better student. It gave my schedule some _____ and I was able to make many friends. And it wasn't just the sports, we also spent a lot of time organizing our club. I think I learned some good life _____ from watching how the senior members did things.

balance
skills
energy
way

🔊 5-06

DISCUSSION   Which one of the survey responses on pages 35 and 36 was most interesting to you? Explain your choice, using the Model Expressions below. Then discuss it with classmates.

I found **A** Sam 's response to be the most **B** interesting . **C** In my experience, ...

A	
1	Sam
2	Stéphanie
3	Catriona
4	Junya

B	
1	surprising
2	bizarre
3	relatable
4	ideal

C	
1	In my experience, ...
2	I had always assumed that ...
3	In my school days, ...
4	If you ask me, ...

....
....
....

VOCABULARY
1. overwhelmingly
2. to impact ~
3. right from the outset
4. test time
5. all the way through to ~
6. to organize ~
7. bizarre
8. ideal
9. I had always assumed that ...

*A father and son who live in Japan responded to the Ibunka Survey. Read about their experience of the son's club activities, and then mark the statements **true** or **false**.*

Father

⑦ My son was a member of the soccer club in junior high school. He was pretty good at it, but in his final year it took up a lot of his time- about 17 hours per week! That's almost half of the hours in a school week in Holland. I felt that it was excessive for a student his age, especially with his grades not being very good at all.

🔊 5-07

Dirk
Dutch professor, lives in Japan

⑨ I went to speak with the coach. I told him that it was unfair that my son would be punished by being excluded from games. It obviously fell on deaf ears. He told me that the club was for "gambaru hito," that is, students who were willing to give their all. I was quite indignant.

🔊 5-09

⑧ My father encouraged me to stay at home on Sundays and rest. I did from time to time, but the coach always punished me for sometimes not coming to practices. He said, "Since you are not really involved in the team, you won't be playing!" I was made to sit out matches and just watch my teammates play.

🔊 5-08

Son

⑩ My father and my coach obviously had very different views on this. As for me, since I wasn't included in games, I lost my desire to play and quit the club. I later joined one which was more relaxed, with only two practices per week.

🔊 5-10

Jakob
Japanese-Dutch student, lives in Japan

	True	False
⑦ Dirk felt that his son was being asked to give an unreasonable amount of time to his soccer club.	☐	☐
⑧ Jakob wasn't allowed to play in matches because he wasn't good enough at soccer.	☐	☐
⑨ After discussion, Jakob's coach was able to see the situation from Jakob's father's point of view.	☐	☐
⑩ Jakob joined a different club after his time at the soccer club ended.	☐	☐

CREATIVITY

Draw a simple manga based on the topic of this unit. It may be from your experience or your imagination.

1	2

3	4

VOCABULARY
1. excessive
2. grades
3. from time to time
4. to be excluded from ~
5. to fall on deaf ears
6. to give one's all
7. indignant
8. to punish
9. involved
10. to be made to sit out
11. obviously
12. to lose the desire to ~

6 In a Shop

In shops and businesses in some cultures, the customer is treated as "royalty". In others, the relationship between staff and customers is more equal. Which do you prefer? Which feels more like "good service" to you?

VOCABULARY   AUDIO   FOR TEACHERS

Part 1 | You and Your Culture

WARM-UP SURVEY *Answer the following questions about your daily life.*

Q1 When you go to a store as a customer, how do you interact with the staff?

	always	sometimes	never
• greet them (or respond to their greeting)	☐	☐	☐
• thank them when you pay?	☐	☐	☐
• make eye contact	☐	☐	☐
• smile	☐	☐	☐
• say something when you leave the store	☐	☐	☐

Q2 As a customer in a store, what do you expect staff to do? → *choose three*

- use polite language ☐
- bow ☐
- smile ☐
- make eye contact ☐
- explain the product / item ☐
- bag / wrap your item carefully ☐
- see you to the door ☐

Q3 Do you enjoy having conversations with shop staff?

- Yes, I enjoy the human interaction. ☐
- Yes, but not for too long and not too often. ☐
- No, I like to keep conversation to a minimum. ☐
- No, I choose shops where I don't have to talk. ☐

Q4 As a customer, which of these do you prefer?

- Being treated with deference, like "royalty." ☐
- Being treated in a friendly manner. ☐

Q5 As a customer, have you ever experienced any of these?

- You received the wrong item or order. ☐
- Something you ordered was not delivered on time. ☐
- Something you ordered was broken or defective. ☐
- A phone operator didn't give you the information you wanted. ☐
- A phone operator was rude to you. ☐

As a shop staff member, have you ever experienced either of these?

- A customer was rude to you. ☐
- A customer got angry at you. ☐

VOCABULARY

1. to interact with ~
2. to greet ~
3. to respond to a greeting
4. to expect ~ to ~
5. to bow
6. to bag (wrap) an item
7. to see ~ to the door
8. human interaction
9. to keep ~ to a minimum
10. deference
11. defective
12. to be rude to ~
13. to get angry at ~

1. First, write your answers to Questions 1~5 in full sentences, giving reasons and opinions where you can.

Q1: When you go to a store as a customer, how do you interact with the staff?

....

....

Q2: As a customer in a store, what do you expect staff to do?

....

....

Q3: Do you enjoy having conversations with shop staff?

....

....

Q4: In a shop, do you prefer to be treated with deference, or to be treated in a friendly manner?

....

....

Q5: Have you ever had an unpleasant experience as a customer or shop staff member?

....

....

2. Ask the survey questions to three classmates and make notes of their answers.

	Q1	Q2	Q3	Q4	Q5
Example Name: *Tomoki*	• makes eye contact • usually responds to greetings	• Expects polite language, bows	• yes, but not too long	• prefers to be treated with deference	• as customer: ordered item was broken • as staff: rude customers
Partner 1 Name:					
Partner 2 Name:					
Partner 3 Name:					

Now let's think about Japanese society and some differences between various groups. Write sentences using words and phrases from these lists.

cafes	**1.** I think that in Japan, customers tend to [____]	ask for a discount
high-end brand stores	[_____] in	expect quality service
hair salons	[_____] more than	chat
bars	they do in [_____].	stay a long time
convenience stores		say hello (goodbye)
family-owned stores	**2.** Staff in [_____] are	say thank you
department stores	more likely to [_____]	talk about themselves
chain restaurants	than those in [_____].	make eye contact
street markets	**3.**	smile

How about you? Are you like most others in Japan, or do you have different views? Write more sentences about Japanese society, adding your own opinions or habits.

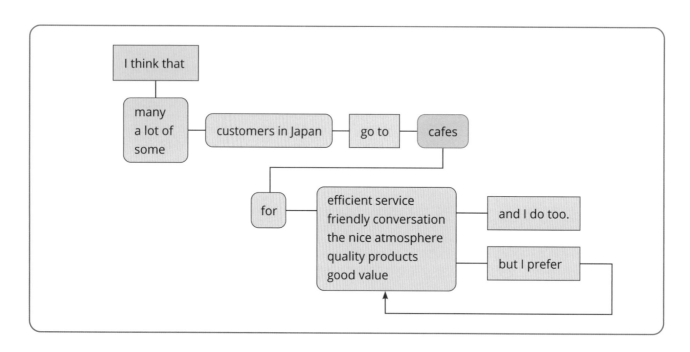

VOCABULARY
1. high-end brand stores
2. hair salons
3. family-owned stores
4. a discount
5. quality service
6. efficient
7. the atmosphere
8. good value
9. I prefer ...

Part 2　People in Other Cultures

People from a range of cultural backgrounds responded to the Ibunka Survey on this topic. Here are a few of their responses for you to read and think about. You will find more in the One Step Further section.

Q1 In the country where you grew up, how do shop staff and customers greet and interact with each other? What about in foreign countries where you have lived?

Jim
Australian,
web designer,
lives in Japan

① In Australia it is very common for customers to reply to shop staff when they greet you. If you don't, you might come across as rude. I don't think this is the case in Japan. I don't see many people return greetings to staff here.

🔊 6-01

② When I was living in rural France, I soon learned to greet everyone, including other customers, when entering a shop. This is not what people did in the industrial town in the UK where I grew up.

🔊 6-02

Kevin
British,
teacher,
has lived in France

Sarah
Canadian,
homemaker, has
lived in Japan

③ Sales staff in Canada often believe that greeting people in a friendly, more casual manner leads to a better customer relationship. So, many retail workers welcome customers with a friendly greeting and try to engage them in conversation.

🔊 6-03

COMPREHENSION 1　*Read the responses and mark the statements **true** or **false**.*

		True	False
❶	Jim is a little shocked by the rudeness of some shop staff in Japan.	☐	☐
❷	Kevin found that shop greetings are more common in France than in his home country.	☐	☐
❸	According to Sarah, it's common for sales staff in Canada to chat with their customers.	☐	☐

VOCABULARY
1.　this is the case
2.　to come across as ~
3.　rural
4.　industrial
5.　retail workers
6.　to engage ~ in conversation

> **Q3** **How do you feel about customer service in your home country?**
> **How about in foreign countries where you have lived?**

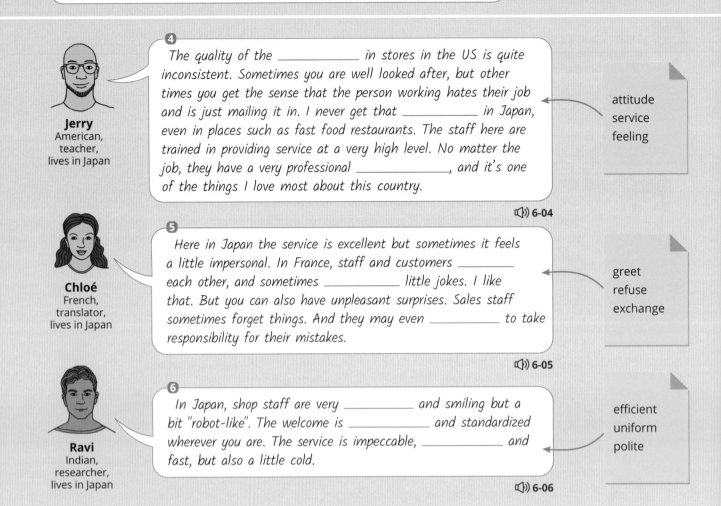

Jerry
American,
teacher,
lives in Japan

④
The quality of the _____ in stores in the US is quite inconsistent. Sometimes you are well looked after, but other times you get the sense that the person working hates their job and is just mailing it in. I never get that _____ in Japan, even in places such as fast food restaurants. The staff here are trained in providing service at a very high level. No matter the job, they have a very professional _____, and it's one of the things I love most about this country.

🔊 6-04

attitude
service
feeling

Chloé
French,
translator,
lives in Japan

⑤
Here in Japan the service is excellent but sometimes it feels a little impersonal. In France, staff and customers _____ each other, and sometimes _____ little jokes. I like that. But you can also have unpleasant surprises. Sales staff sometimes forget things. And they may even _____ to take responsibility for their mistakes.

🔊 6-05

greet
refuse
exchange

Ravi
Indian,
researcher,
lives in Japan

⑥
In Japan, shop staff are very _____ and smiling but a bit "robot-like". The welcome is _____ and standardized wherever you are. The service is impeccable, _____ and fast, but also a little cold.

🔊 6-06

efficient
uniform
polite

DISCUSSION *Which one of the survey responses on pages 41 and 42 was most interesting to you? Explain your choice, using the patterns below as a starting point. Then discuss it with classmates.*

I found **Jim** [A] 's response to be the most **surprising** [B]. **In my experience, ...** [C]

A			
1	Jim	5	Émilie
2	Kevin	6	Ravi
3	Sarah		
4	Jerry		

B	
1	surprising
2	fascinating
3	relatable
4	shocking

C	
1	In my experience, ...
2	In my culture, ...
3	From my point of view, ...
4	I'm most comfortable with ...

VOCABULARY
1. inconsistent
2. to mail it in
3. no matter the ~
4. impersonal
5. to take responsibility for ~
6. standardized
7. impeccable

7

I remember being quite surprised by a few things when I visited a souk market in Morocco. The stall-holders were quite aggressive, holding the arms of passers-by and guiding them into their shops. But once I was inside, I enjoyed the interaction with the stall-holder. He sat me down, poured me some tea, and we had a nice chat before he even started talking about products and prices. I guess in a culture where you haggle over prices, personal conversation is a good way to begin.

Gus
Irish,
actor,
lives in Spain

🔊 6-07

8

I sometimes get reverse culture shock when I go back to France on holiday. I have gotten used to the politeness and thoughtfulness of the Japanese. Back in France, one day, while paying at the checkout of a supermarket, it seemed to me that the cashier had been rude. I told her, "You could speak politely." A customer standing in line behind me defended her by saying, "But she <u>was</u> polite." I was shocked!

Catherine
French,
architect,
lives in Japan

🔊 6-08

	True	False
7 Gus was most surprised at the price of tea in the market in Morocco.	☐	☐
8 Catherine's idea of "polite service" changed while she was living in a foreign culture.	☐	☐

CREATIVITY   *Draw a simple manga based on the topic of this unit. It may be from your experience or your imagination.*

1	2

3	4

VOCABULARY
1. stall-holders
2. aggressive
3. interaction
4. passers-by
5. to haggle over ~
6. reverse culture shock
7. thoughtfulness
8. checkout
9. cashier

Romance and Relationships

What kinds of things do you find romantic? How should partners in a relationship behave towards each other? How about when in the presence of others? The answers to these questions may seem "natural," but in fact they are deeply cultural.

VOCABULARY   AUDIO   FOR TEACHERS

Part 1   You and Your Culture

WARM-UP SURVEY   *Answer the following questions about your daily life.*

WARM-UP SURVEY

Q1 **What kinds of actions do you think are romantic?** → *choose three*

- giving flowers or small gifts ☐
- dinner for two at a fancy restaurant ☐
- doing the dishes for your partner ☐
- a day trip to Disneyland ☐
- little messages of love ☐
- a cooked breakfast ☐
- remembering your anniversaries ☐
- other: ....

Q2 **Which of these do you think is a stronger sign of love between partners?**

- talking openly and honestly about most things ☐
- being able to notice or guess your partner's needs without words ☐

Q3 **Imagine you are on a lunch date with someone. Who pays the bill?**

- Me. ☐
- My partner. ☐
- We split the bill. ☐

Q4 **Imagine you are going to get married or live with someone. What things do you think are important to do together with your partner?**

	important	not important
talk about your day	☐	☐
eat dinner together	☐	☐
make big decisions	☐	☐
go on regular dates	☐	☐
have friends in common	☐	☐

- other: ....

Q5 **Would you like to get married or live with a partner in the future? Why or why not?**

- Yes. I would like to get married because :
  - I want to share my life with someone. ☐
  - I want to have kids. ☐
  - other: ....
- No. I don't think I'll get married because :
  - I want to keep my freedom. ☐
  - I want to be independent. ☐
  - other: ....
- It depends on:
  - whether or not I find the right person ☐
  - my financial situation ☐
  - my family situation ☐
  - other: ....

VOCABULARY
1. fancy
2. to do the dishes
3. to talk openly
4. your partner's needs
5. to split the bill
6. whether or not

1. First, write your answers to Questions 1~5 in full sentences, giving reasons and opinions where you can.

Q1: What kinds of actions do you think are romantic?

....

....

Q2: Which of these do you think is more important in a relationship: to talk openly and honestly about most things, or to be able to notice your partner's needs without words?

....

....

Q3: Who usually pays the bill when you are on a lunch date with someone?

....

....

Q4: What kinds of things do you think are important to do together with your long-term partner?

....

....

Q5: Would you like to get married (or live with someone) in the future?

....

....

2. Ask the survey questions to three classmates and make notes of their answers.

	Q1	Q2	Q3	Q4	Q5
Example Name: *Sakura*	• *give little gifts* • *messages*	• *guessing your partner's needs*	• *split the bill*	• *talk about your day* • *regular dates*	• *yes, wants to get married in late twenties* • *wants to have kids*
Partner 1 Name:					
Partner 2 Name:					
Partner 3 Name:					

Now let's think about Japanese society and some differences between various groups. Write sentences using words and phrases from these lists.

young couples	**1.** I think that in Japan, [____]	share the housework
middle-aged couples	[____] tend to	go on regular dates
elderly couples	[____].	talk openly about everything
couples in urban areas	**2.** I have the feeling that [____]	guess their partner's needs
couples in rural areas	[____] are more likely to [____]	both have jobs
conservative types	[____] than [____]	have traditional gender roles
progressive types	[____].	live together before marriage
men	**3.**	hold hands in public
women	....	wear matching 'pair look' clothes

How about you? Are you like most others in Japan, or do you have different views? Write more sentences about Japanese society, adding your own opinions or habits.

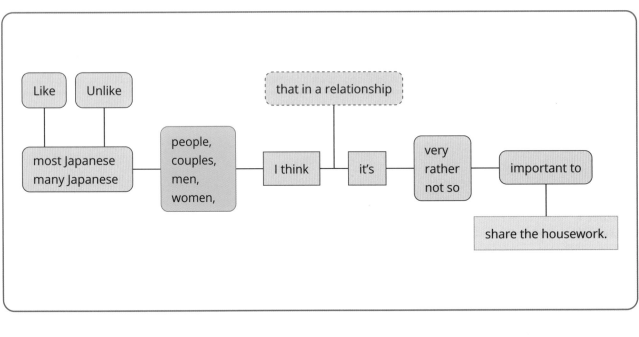

Like / Unlike — most Japanese / many Japanese — people, couples, men, women, — I think — that in a relationship — it's — very / rather / not so — important to — share the housework.

....

....

....

....

....

....

....

VOCABULARY
1. conservative types
2. progressive types
3. to be likely to ~
4. to share the housework
5. regular
6. traditional gender roles
7. "pair-look" clothes

People from a range of cultural backgrounds responded to the Ibunka Survey on this topic. Here are a few of their responses for you to read and think about. You will find more in the One Step Further section.

ibunka SURVEY

Q1   In your opinion, is it OK for couples to have public displays of affection?

Nadia
Italian,
teacher and
translator,
lives in Japan

1 My Japanese husband is OK with holding hands when we walk around together, but he is not OK with kissing me on the street. I sometimes miss a quick peck on the cheek.

🔊 **7-01**

2 I know some people may find it embarrassing, but I feel it is natural for couples to show their affection at any time. It shouldn't matter where you are. I am very proud of my wife and I am happy to allow people to see that I love her very much.

🔊 **7-02**

Trevor
American,
businessman,
has lived in
the UK

3 When I was a student in the US, I found it very strange that people called me romantic all the time just because of my French nationality.

🔊 **7-03**

Jacques
French,
surveyor,
has lived in the US

4 And in fact, I was shocked whenever I went out with couples. Often they were all over each other, holding each other, kissing, and calling each other cute names. In France, that behavior is considered quite rude by people you are with (your friends or your family), as if you are excluding them or ignoring them.

🔊 **7-04**

COMPREHENSION 1   *Read the responses and mark the statements **true** or **false**.*

		True	False
1	Nadia's husband likes to express his love for her with kisses when they go out together.	☐	☐
2	Trevor doesn't see anything wrong with showing affection towards his wife in front of others.	☐	☐
3	Jacques is a true romantic, but people in the US didn't recognize that.	☐	☐
4	Jacques felt that American couples' public behavior was inappropriate.	☐	☐

VOCABULARY
1. public displays of affection
2. to walk around
3. peck on the cheek
4. at any time
5. It shouldn't matter where ~
6. to be all over each other
7. to call each other cute names
8. to exclude
9. to ignore
10. inappropriate

Q2 Do you think it's important that couples discuss everything, or should people be able to understand their partner's needs without words?

5

Hanna
Hungarian,
research student,
lives in Japan

I would say that discussion is definitely important. In Hungary, we have a proverb that says, "Even a mother can't _____ the words of a speechless child." Basically, this means that we shouldn't _____ anyone to guess our needs if we don't _____ them into words. I think that being able to _____ to each other's opinions and requests is one of the most vital things in a relationship.

listen
understand
expect
put

🔊 7-05

6

Maho
Japanese,
office worker,
has lived in Brazil

My Brazilian _____ asks me to tell him, exactly what I want, but I wish he could "read the _____" a little better. I know there are cultural _____, but I feel that if he truly loves me, he should take the _____ to notice my needs.

signs
time
partner
differences

🔊 7-06

DISCUSSION *Which one of the survey responses on pages 47 and 48 was most interesting to you? Explain your choice, using the patterns below as a starting point. Then discuss it with classmates.*

I found [A] Nadia 's response to be the most [B] interesting . Ideally, I think that people in a relationship should [C] ...

A	
1	Nadia
2	Trevor
3	Jacques
4	Hanna
5	Maho

B	
1	interesting
2	debatable
3	unexpected
4	realistic

C	
1	Ideally, I think that people in a relationship should ...
2	It seems strange to me that ...
3	Personally, ...
4	In my experience ...

....

....

....

....

....

....

....

VOCABULARY
1. I would say that ~
2. definitely
3. speechless
4. to put ~ into words
5. vital
6. realistic
7. ideally

*An international couple living in Japan has responded to the Ibunka Survey. As you will see, they have different opinions about how a couple should talk about decisions they need to make. Read their responses and mark the statements **true** or **false**.*

Wife

Mila
Swiss,
cabin attendant,
lives in Japan

7 *When I met my Japanese boyfriend (who later became my husband), I thought we could have frank discussions about anything. But that was before we got serious.*

🔊 **7-07**

8 *I am fine with discussing things, but in a truly loving relationship, both partners ought to be attentive to the other's needs and feelings. I feel that without real empathy, talk is useless.*

🔊 **7-08**

9 *For me, it's only after having a good discussion that you can really empathize with someone. If you just try to guess their feelings, the chances are high that you'll be mistaken a lot of the time.*

🔊 **7-09**

10 *My wife and I are both supposed to be adults. So I feel that I shouldn't have to explain everything to her. But when we need to make a decision, she insists on discussing everything in detail. I sometimes feel that she is like a robot that can't deal with real human emotions. It's frustrating, but we're both making an effort to bridge the gap.*

Husband

Takeru
Japanese,
designer,
has lived
in Switzerland

🔊 **7-10**

	True	False
7 Takeru wanted Mila to tell him all about her ex-boyfriend Frank.	☐	☐
8 Takeru believes that true love must include being aware of what your partner needs.	☐	☐
9 Mila is confident that she can always guess what Takeru is thinking.	☐	☐
10 Takeru's wife can explain in detail how robots work.	☐	☐

Draw a simple manga based on the topic of this unit. It may be from your experience or your imagination.

1	2

3	4

VOCABULARY
1. ought to ~
2. to be attentive to ~
3. empathy
4. to empathize with ~
5. the chances are high that ~
6. to be mistaken
7. a lot of the time
8. to deal with
9. frustrating
10. to bridge a gap

Conversation and Discussion

When having a conversation with someone, do you usually "take small steps" with what you say, or are you more upfront about your thoughts and opinions? When discussing a topic, how comfortable are you with having and expressing different perspectives?

VOCABULARY   AUDIO   FOR TEACHERS

Part 1   You and Your Culture

WARM-UP SURVEY   *Answer the following questions about your daily life.*

WARM-UP SURVEY

Q1   Which of the following topics do you enjoy talking about? → *choose three*

- hobbies ☐
- values and beliefs ☐
- news and current events ☐
- politics ☐
- art / pop culture ☐
- sport ☐
- fashion ☐
- the lives of famous people ☐
- Internet content (YouTube, Instagram, etc) ☐
- life goals and dreams ☐
- other: ....

Q2   Imagine that someone you didn't know well asked you, "Do you have a part-time job?" Which of these two ways of answering would be more natural to you?

- "No, I don't." ☐
- "No, I used to, but I don't have the time anymore. I'd like to work at a cafe again in the future." ☐

Q3   Imagine that you are discussing the topic of "the best place to live in Japan." You give your honest opinion, but the person you are talking with disagrees with you completely, giving reasons. Which emotion are you more likely to feel?

- Shocked because someone has hurt my feelings. ☐
- Excited by the idea of a lively discussion. ☐

Q4   Do you ever discuss abstract topics with friends? (for example: "What is the meaning of life?", "How important is freedom?", etc.)

- Yes, often. ☐
- Sometimes. ☐
- Yes, but rarely. ☐
- No, never. ☐

Q5   What do you find most uncomfortable when having a conversation or discussion with someone? → *choose three*

- lack of eye contact ☐
- too much eye contact ☐
- long silences ☐
- boring topics ☐
- no interest shown in what you say ☐
- being interrupted ☐
- aggressiveness ☐
- not knowing what someone is actually thinking ☐
- people speaking too much about themselves ☐
- people who don't express their true opinions ☐

VOCABULARY
1. to be upfront about ~
2. (different) perspectives
3. values
4. beliefs
5. current events
6. abstract
7. lack of ~
8. being interrupted
9. aggressiveness

1. First, write your answers to Questions 1~5 in full sentences, giving reasons and opinions where you can.

Q1: What topics do you most enjoy talking about?

....

....

Q2: In reponse to simple questions, do you usually give short answers or longer ones?

....

....

Q3: How do you feel when someone disagrees with you openly?

....

....

Q4: Do you ever discuss abstract topics with others?

....

....

Q5: What kinds of behavior do you find uncomfortable when you are talking with someone?

....

....

2. Ask the survey questions to several classmates and make notes of their answers.

	Q1	Q2	Q3	Q4	Q5
Example Name: *Yoshito*	• *sports* • *hobbies* • *Internet*	• *tend to give short answers*	• *shocked (hurt feelings)*	• *Yes, but only rarely*	• *boring topics* • *no interest in what I'm saying* • *aggressiveness*
Partner 1 Name:					
Partner 2 Name:					
Partner 3 Name:					

Now let's think about Japanese society and some differences between various groups. Write sentences using words and phrases from these lists.

men
women
people who have lived abroad
creative people
people from Kansai
people from Kanto
elderly people
young people

1. I feel that within Japanese society, [_____]

[_____] are better at [_____]

[_____] than [_____] are.

2. In my experience, [_____]

[_____] tend to be good at [_____]

[_____].

3. ....

....

....

expressing an opinion
leading a discussion
disagreeing politely
speaking actively
making a point
listening to others
reaching agreement
speaking in public

How about you? Are you like most others in Japan, or do you have different views? Write more sentences about Japanese society, adding your own opinions or habits.

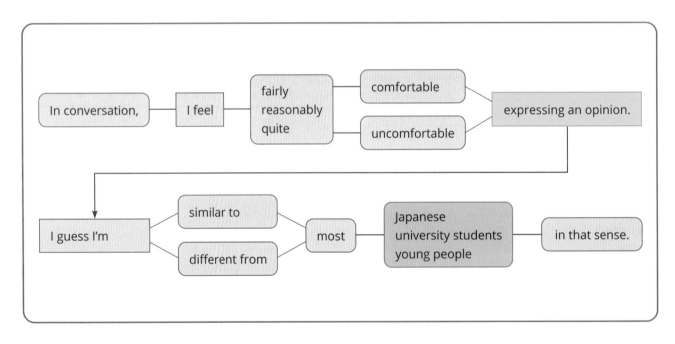

....

....

....

....

....

....

....

VOCABULARY
1. creative people
2. to lead a discussion
3. to disagree politely
4. to make a point
5. to reach agreement
6. fairly
7. comfortable
8. in that sense

People from a range of cultural backgrounds responded to the Ibunka Survey on this topic. Here are a few of their responses for you to read and think about. You will find more in the One Step Further section.

ibunka SURVEY

Q1 **Imagine that someone you don't know well asks you the question, "Do you have a part-time job?" Would you naturally give a short answer (for example "No, I don't.")? Or would you volunteer a longer answer? (for example "No, I used to, but I don't have the time any more. I'd like to work at a cafe again in the future.")**

Mark
American,
professor,
lives in Japan,
has lived in
Mexico and France

❶ *Short answers like, "No, I don't" seem rather cold to me. It feels like the person answering wants to end the conversation. By not adding something, like a question or more information, there seems to be no interest in communicating.*

🔊 8-01

❷ *If I don't feel like continuing the conversation, I'm more likely to answer quite dryly and briefly. I think most Europeans give longer answers to show that they are open to conversation, or simply say, "No, what about you?"*

🔊 8-02

Ulrike
German,
accountant,
lives in Japan

❸ *But in Japan, when people give an answer as short as, "No, I don't", it doesn't necessarily mean they don't want to talk. You have to "read the air" to pick up on other signs that encourage discussion.*

🔊 8-03

Takato
Japanese,
engineer,
has lived in Australia
and the UAE

❹ *Living abroad, I found that Australians give pretty long responses, but those I met in the UAE (including Arab people, Indians and Bangladeshis) tend to reply quite minimally.*

🔊 8-04

COMPREHENSION 1 *Read the responses and mark the statements **true** or **false**.*

		True	False
❶	Mark feels that giving longer answers is part of active communication.	☐	☐
❷	Ulrike says that Europeans give long answers because they only want to make the conversation about themselves.	☐	☐
❸	Ulrike believes that in Japan, people who give short answers are showing that they don't want to talk.	☐	☐
❹	Takato experienced two similar response styles in the two foreign countries he lived in.	☐	☐

VOCABULARY
1. the person answering
2. dryly
3. not necessarily
4. to encourage ~
5. to pick up on ~
6. UAE
7. minimally

Q2   **Do you like to discuss abstract topics with others? If you do, are you comfortable with disagreeing with your discussion partner(s), or do you prefer to look for agreement and common ground?**

Juri
Japanese,
homemaker,
has lived in France

5 *I am married to a Frenchman. A long time ago, when he was my boyfriend, he invited a French acquaintance to our place. They started to _____ politics and the conversation got quite heated. I thought they were fighting, and I started to _____ ! They were very surprised. They said, "We are just having fun, don't worry!" On that day I learnt that French people _____ a good debate. For them, disagreeing is sometimes more fun than agreeing. They don't _____ it personally.*

enjoy
take
discuss
cry

🔊 8-05

Andrew
Australian,
actor,
has lived in France

6 *I'm probably more comfortable in the _____ I grew up in. However, I did appreciate the directness of the French, and their _____ of seeing disagreement not as a personal _____ but as an essential and respectful way of making _____. In Australia, disagreement can often be seen as disrespectful and quite arrogant, I think.*

attack
way
culture
conversation

🔊 8-06

DISCUSSION   *Which one of the survey responses on pages 53 and 54 was most interesting to you? Explain your choice, using the patterns below as a starting point. Then discuss it with classmates.*

I found **A** Mark 's response to be the most **B** controversial . **C** For me, the best kind of conversation is ...

	A
1	Mark
2	Ulrike
3	Takato
4	Juri
5	Andrew

	B
1	interesting
2	unusual
3	controversial
4	relatable

	C
1	In my view …
2	It's hard to believe that …
3	In my culture, …
4	For me, the best kind of conversation is …

VOCABULARY
1. abstract
2. common ground
3. acquaintance
4. directness
5. to be seen as ~
6. disrespectful
7. arrogant
8. controversial

❼ When I lived in the US, I was told to stop interrupting other people during a discussion, because it was rude. It was so shocking for me to hear that. It was as if I were a bad-mannered person! In Italy, we often "jump into a discussion" when we are interested in what someone is saying.

🔊 8-07

Vincenzo
Italian,
data analyst,
has lived in the US

❽ I got the sense that Americans make a point of not interrupting each other. They speak on and on, and they don't even look at you to see if you are interested in what they are saying. That kind of discussion felt rather boring to me.

🔊 8-08

		True	False
❼	Vincenzo was surprised that people in the US thought his behavior was rude.	☐	☐
❽	Vincenzo is convinced that Americans interrupt each other all the time.	☐	☐

VOCABULARY
1. bad-mannered
2. to jump into ~
3. to get the sense that ~
4. to make a point of ~
5. on and on

CREATIVITY   *Draw a simple manga based on the topic of this unit. It may be from your experience or your imagination.*

1	2

3	4

9 Parents and Children

How children are raised is very much a cultural matter. In some cultures, the predominant view is that children must be supported, encouraged and protected. In other cultures, the emphasis is on children learning society's rules as early as possible.

VOCABULARY AUDIO FOR TEACHERS

Part 1 You and Your Culture

WARM-UP SURVEY *Please answer the following questions about your daily life.* WARM-UP SURVEY

Q1 Did you ever sleep in the same bed as your parents? Until what age?
- Yes, until age .... ☐
- No, I never did. ☐

Q2 What do you think is the most appropriate bedtime for a six-year-old child?
- around .... o'clock.

Q3 For you, when was the most enjoyable stage of your childhood?
- before elementary school (up to age 6) ☐
- elementary school (ages 6 - 12) ☐
- junior high school (ages 12 -15) ☐
- senior high school (ages 15 -18) ☐

Q4 In your opinion, is it acceptable for a five-year old child to...

	OK	Not OK
• interrupt adults who are speaking among themselves?	☐	☐
• have no table manners?	☐	☐
• be noisy in public places?	☐	☐
• choose the family dinner menu?	☐	☐

Q5 In your opinion, when a couple has a baby, do you think it's normal that their life becomes centered on their child?
- Yes, because ...
  - the best gift that parents can give to a child is to support them 100%. ☐
  - small children always need their parents' help. ☐
  - children need to be constantly encouraged. ☐
  - children need lots of skinship and intimacy. ☐
  - other: ....
- No, because ...
  - parents need time and space to maintain their relationship as a couple. ☐
  - parents also need to have a healthy social life. ☐
  - happy parents means happy children. ☐
  - other: ....

VOCABULARY
1. to be raised
2. predominant
3. the emphasis is on ~
4. appropriate
5. stage
6. to interrupt ~
7. among themselves
8. table manners

1. First, write your answers to Questions 1~5 in full sentences, giving reasons and opinions where you can.

Q1: Did you ever sleep in the same bed as your parents? If so, until what age?

....

....

Q2: What do you think is the most appropriate bedtime for a six-year-old child?

....

....

Q3: For you, when was the most enjoyable stage of your childhood?

....

....

Q4: In your opinion, is it acceptable for a five-year-old child to interrupt adults? (to have no table manners? / to be noisy in public places? / to choose the family dinner menu?)

....

....

Q5: In your opinion, when a couple has a baby, do you think it's normal that their life becomes centered on that child?

....

....

2. Ask the survey questions to several classmates and make notes of their answers.

	Q1	Q2	Q3	Q4	Q5
Example Name: *Miki*	• 7 years old	• around 9pm	• elementary school- had most freedom	• Interrupt adults: OK • No table manners: Not OK • Noisy in public: not OK • Choose menu: OK	• Yes, small children always need their parents' help / attention
Partner 1 Name:					
Partner 2 Name:					
Partner 3 Name:					

Now let's think about Japanese society and some differences between various groups. Write sentences using words and phrases from these lists.

parents of preschoolers
parents of elementary school children
parents of junior high school students
parents of high school students
parents of boys
parents of girls
working mothers
stay-at-home mothers

1. I have the feeling that ⬚

⬚ are quite strict

about ⬚.

2. In my view, ⬚

⬚ tend to be more lenient about

⬚ than they are about

⬚.

3. ....
....
....

bedtime
study
academic success
extracurricular activities
good behavior in public
table manners
respect for others

How about you? Are you like most others in Japan, or do you have different views? Write more sentences about Japanese society, adding your own opinions or habits.

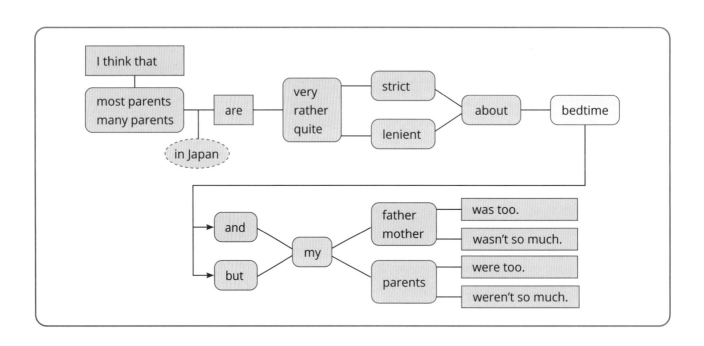

....
....
....
....
....
....
....

VOCABULARY
1. preschoolers
2. stay-at-home mothers
3. strict
4. lenient
5. academic success
6. extracurricular activities
7. respect for others

People from a range of cultural backgrounds responded to the Ibunka Survey on this topic. Here are a few of their responses for you to read and think about. You will find more in the One Step Further section.

ibunka SURVEY

Q1 Until what age did you sleep in the same bed as your parents (if you did)?

Bill
American,
surveyor,
has lived in Mexico

❶ I probably never slept in the same bed as my parents. I was put in a crib from a very young age. Then my parents probably put the crib and me in another room very soon after that, when I was just a few months old. In my country, privacy for parents is very important. The parents' bed should remain a place for the couple, not for the family.

🔊 **9-01**

❷ In the UK, many people think that if little children sleep in the same bed as their parents they will never "cut the cord," that is, become fully independent from their parents. So it's largely frowned upon.

🔊 **9-02**

Catriona
British,
writer,
lives in Japan

❸ Since I started living in Japan, my thoughts on children having their own rooms has changed. I used to think they should sleep in a separate room from birth, but later I came to think that this should happen when they start school. Now, I think it should be only when they feel ready. Sleeping with my kids was so cozy and intimate.

🔊 **9-03**

COMPREHENSION 1 Read the responses and mark the statements **true** or **false**.

		True	False
❶	Bill slept in a separate room from his parents' from when he was born.	☐	☐
❷	In the UK, it's widely believed that sleeping with your children is not good for their development.	☐	☐
❸	Through experience, Catriona found that there were good points to co-sleeping.	☐	☐

VOCABULARY
1. crib
2. privacy
3. to cut the cord
4. fully independent
5. to be frowned upon
6. co-sleeping

Q2 In the culture you grew up in, would you say that the general attitude toward children is strict? How about in other cultures you have lived in?

Julien
French,
teacher,
lives in Japan

④

It seems _____ to me that in Japan there is a real laissez-faire attitude of parents towards their children! I often see children whining in front of other people, and their _____ parents say nothing. French children usually behave themselves in public. If they are _____ or boisterous they will be quickly reprimanded.

🔊 **9-04**

noisy
unconcerned
obvious

Tim
Australian,
artist,
has lived
in France

⑤

I lived in France for a few years. I would say that children there seemed to be better behaved than children in Australia. I think in France the expectations were higher, and there were fewer _____ made for children who weren't behaving in a socially acceptable way.

🔊 **9-05**

⑥

Here in Australia, I think there's a _____ for the child to always be seen as 'right' in the eyes of their parents, and this is played out in parents' _____ with teachers and _____ in schools across the country. I would say that children in my culture are supported almost to the point of being indulged.

🔊 **9-06**

tendency
excuses
relationships
discipline

DISCUSSION   Which one of the survey responses on pages 59 and 60 was most interesting to you? Explain your choice, using the patterns below as a starting point. Then discuss it with classmates.

I found [A] Bill 's response to be the most [B] thought-provoking. When I was a child, I ... [C]

A	
1	Bill
2	Catriona
3	Julien
4	Tim

B	
1	thought-provoking
2	debatable
3	unexpected
4	realistic

C	
1	When I was a child, I ...
2	It seems strange to me that ...
3	Personally, ...
4	In my experience ...

VOCABULARY
1. laissez-faire
2. whining
3. unconcerned
4. to behave oneself
5. boisterous
6. (high) expectations
7. in the eyes of ~
8. to be reprimanded
9. to be played out

Read the responses and mark the statements **true** or **false**.

Q3 Have you noticed any differences in parenting between your home culture and other cultures you have lived in?

Jennifer
Canadian,
homemaker,
lives in Japan

❼ I get the impression that mothers in Japan are expected to devote all of their time and energy to their children. It seems that they almost stop being individuals while they are raising their children, and only get their life back when the kids leave the nest. But maybe it's less true of the younger generation.

🔊 9-07

❽ I have always been struck by how much some Japanese parents pamper their children. I see my wife's relatives sleeping in the same bed as their kids, preparing their meals, even letting them choose the family dinner menu. I sometimes worry that these children will never learn any responsibility.

🔊 9-08

Rick,
New Zealander,
teacher,
lives in Japan

❾ But once they leave the house, these same kids are amazingly mature. Many small children walk by themselves to school, and carry out many duties in their classrooms, such as serving lunches and cleaning the school. This gap between indulgence and discipline is pretty startling for many Westerners I've spoken to.

🔊 9-09

	True	False
❼ Jennifer thinks that many Japanese mothers don't put enough energy into their parenting.	☐	☐
❽ Rick believes that parents shouldn't let children choose what to have for dinner.	☐	☐
❾ Seeing young children clean their own schools was surprising to Rick.	☐	☐

CREATIVITY Draw a simple manga *based on the topic of this unit. It may be from your experience or your imagination.*

1	2

3	4

VOCABULARY
1. individuals
2. to get one's life back
3. to leave the nest
4. to pamper ~
5. responsibility
6. to carry out duties
7. mature
8. indulgence
9. discipline
10. startling

Asking someone to do a favor is tricky even in your own culture, but when the person you are asking has a different idea of how this should be done, it can be even more difficult. The way we use language to manage social obligations is quite unique to each culture.

VOCABULARY   AUDIO   FOR TEACHERS

Part 1 | You and Your Culture

WARM-UP SURVEY *Answer the following questions about your daily life.*

WARM-UP SURVEY

Q1 What kind of favors do you ask of people around you? Who do you usually ask?

	family members	close friends	classmates	teachers
• help with study	☐	☐	☐	☐
• help with work	☐	☐	☐	☐
• lend/borrow something	☐	☐	☐	☐
• advice	☐	☐	☐	☐
• other:				

Q2 Are you more comfortable asking favors from people older than you, or people younger than you?
→ *rank these groups 1,2,3 in order of most to least comfortable*

people older than you	classmates (same age)	people younger than you

Q3 When you ask someone your own age for a favor, do you ...

- ask directly? ☐
- hint that you have a problem and wait for them to offer help? ☐
- apologize for putting them out? ☐
- promise to do something in return? ☐
- give something in return? ☐

Q4 Think about your best friend from high school. Which of these favors would you be comfortable asking of them?

- help with homework ☐
- a lend of a book ☐
- a lend of 10, 000 yen ☐
- advice on love ☐
- putting you up in their home for 3 nights ☐
- other: ....

Q5 When you ask someone for a favor, do you expect that you will have to repay it?

- Absolutely. ☐
- Usually. ☐
- Not really. ☐
- It depends on the person. ☐

VOCABULARY
1. tricky
2. to ask favors of ~
3. close friend
4. to hint
5. to apologize for ~
6. to put ~ out
7. in return
8. to put ~ up
9. to repay
10. It depends on ~

1. First, write your answers to Questions 1~5 in full sentences, giving reasons and opinions where you can.

Q1: What kinds of favors do you ask of people around you? Who do you ask?

....

....

Q2: Are you more comfortable asking favors from people older than you, or younger than you?

....

....

Q3: When you ask someone your age for a favor, how do you go about it?

....

....

Q4: What kinds of favors could you ask of your best friend from high school?

....

....

Q5: When you ask someone for a favor, do you expect that you will have to repay it?

....

....

2. Ask the survey questions to several classmates and make notes of their answers.

	Q1	Q2	Q3	Q4	Q5
Example Name: *Hayato*	• *advice: family, close friends* • *study help: close friends*	• *most comfortable: older people* • *least comfortable: classmates*	• *hint at my problem (usually)*	• *help with homework* • *lend of a book* • *advice on love*	• *Yes, I usually feel that way.*
Partner 1 Name:					
Partner 2 Name:					
Partner 3 Name:					

Now let's think about Japanese society and some differences between various groups. Write sentences using words and phrases from these lists.

close friends		ask directly
co-workers		drop hints instead of asking
classmates		give something in return
senior students		do something in return
junior students		ask close friends
men		ask older people
women		ask family members

1. It's my view that in Japan, _____

_____ _____

for favors more than _____ do.

2. I feel that in Japanese society, _____

_____ often _____

_____ for favors because ....

....

3. ....

....

....

How about you? Are you like most others in Japan, or do you have different views? Write more sentences about Japanese society, adding your own opinions or habits.

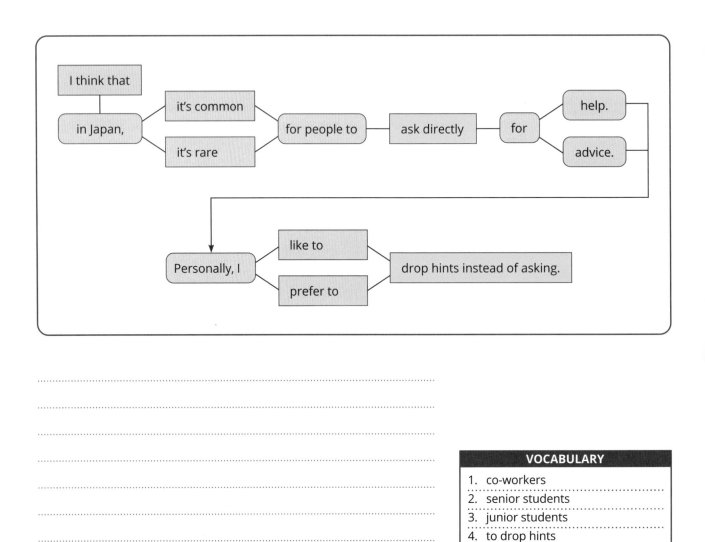

....
....
....
....
....
....
....

VOCABULARY
1. co-workers
2. senior students
3. junior students
4. to drop hints
5. instead of ~

Part 2　People in Other Cultures

People from a range of cultural backgrounds responded to the Ibunka Survey *on this topic. Here are a few of their responses for you to read and think about. You will find more in the* One Step Further *section.*

Q1　An expert on American and French cultures* has observed that Americans tend to directly ask favors of their friends. In contrast, French people tend to indirectly hint at a problem they are having, and wait for their friends to offer help. Does that match your personal experience? How do people do this in the culture you grew up in?

*Raymonde Carroll (see page 96)

Marie
French,
artist,
lives in Japan

❶ As a French person, I agree with the remark concerning French society. When I need help, I tend to just talk to my friends about my problems without asking for help directly, in order to avoid putting pressure on them.

🔊 10-01

❷ I suppose that Americans are rather direct. Especially with people we're close to, we just say, "Hey, could you do me a favor?" or use some other casual expression. And it can be okay to say no to a request without suffering any lasting damage to the relationship.

🔊 10-02

Joey
American,
teacher,
lives in Japan

❸ Australians generally ask favors of others directly but politely. I have the feeling that hinting at a problem might be seen as slippery or even somehow dishonest, since it's generally a culture which prides itself on straight, honest communication.

🔊 10-03

Lesley
Australian,
biologist,
has lived in Japan

❹ In Japan, my experience is that usually it is enough to describe your problem, and the other person will understand that you are asking for help. In that sense, it is the complete opposite of Hungary. In Hungary, if you were to ask a favor simply by describing your situation, you would probably receive a response like "So?" or "I see."

🔊 10-04

Patricia
Hungarian,
student,
lives in Japan

COMPREHENSION 1　*Read the responses and mark the statements **true** or **false**.*

		True	False
❶	Marie believes that asking her friends directly for help would have a negative affect on their relationship.	☐	☐
❷	Joey would probably only ever ask a favor of his friends using very formal language.	☐	☐
❸	According to Lesley, in Australian culture it's probably better to explain honestly what you want when asking for favors.	☐	☐
❹	Patricia says that the way in which people ask for favors in Hungary is exactly the same as in Japan.	☐	☐

VOCABULARY
1. people we're close to
2. lasting damage
3. slippery
4. somehow
5. dishonest
6. to pride oneself on ~
7. the complete opposite of ~

Q2 **In your culture, or the foreign cultures you have lived in, how do people repay the social obligations that come with asking favors or receiving gifts?**

5

In Japan, people keep track of social debt! This is a reason why people _____ presents so often, even when they _____ someone's home. Any sort of imposition must be compensated for. It's a "give and _____" society, as my Japanese wife often says. I guess people are very aware of this, and maybe that's why they don't often _____ for favors.

ask
visit
give
take

🔊 10-05

Jerry
American,
carpenter,
lives in Japan

6

I have the impression that Japanese people tend not to ask for help, probably because it makes them _____ to the person who helped them. And I'm _____ that many Japanese people I know give _____ gifts in return for gifts, favors, or simply putting others out.

generous
conscious
accountable

🔊 10-06

Scott
Australian,
teacher,
lives in Japan, has
lived in the UK

7

In Pakistan, people usually ask directly for favors, but I think we tend to change our _____ depending on what we're asking for, and who we're asking. In return, Pakistani people invite others for a _____ at their home or a restaurant. Or if we go to someone's house, we always take some fruit or _____. There is a strong _____ of returning favors.

sweets
style
ethos
meal

🔊 10-07

Ali
Pakistani,
student,
lives in Japan

DISCUSSION   *Which one of the survey responses on pages 65 and 66 was most interesting to you? Explain your choice, using the patterns below as a starting point. Then discuss it with classmates.*

I found [A] Joey 's response to be the most [B] surprising . [C] I wouldn't have thought that ...

	A		
1	Marie	5	Jerry
2	Joey	6	Scott
3	Lesley	7	Ali
4	Patricia		

	B
1	surprising
2	thought-provoking
3	odd
4	reasonable

	C
1	I wouldn't have thought that ...
2	In my experience ...
3	I find it more natural to ...
4	I agree that it's ...

VOCABULARY
1. social debt
2. imposition
3. to compensate for ~
4. generous
5. conscious
6. accountable
7. ethos

Mariko
Japanese,
editor,
has lived in England

❽   There is a Japanese expression that goes, "A small kindness can incur a big debt for others" (chisa na shinsetsu, ookina sewa). I don't want to make trouble for another person, so I don't want to just thoughtlessly offer my help, and end up burdening them. I only offer help after carefully observing the other person's needs. I am also cautious of offers of help from others, because sometimes their sympathy is only superficial.

🔊 **10-08**

❾   In Japanese, there are euphemistic phrases used to politely turn down an offer of help, which might not be perceived as refusals by people outside of the culture. For example, "I'll consider it," "That sounds OK," or "That might be a good idea." I feel that this kind of language sometimes leads to misunderstandings when translated directly into English.

Yoshi
Japanese,
JICA overseas volunteer,
has lived in Nepal

🔊 **10-09**

Juan
Mexican,
teacher,
lives in Japan

❿   I find that after spending an extended period of time in Japan I have come to apologize a lot when asking for favors or help, even when I speak my native language. It's almost like a default setting of humility and politeness.

🔊 **10-10**

		True	False
❽	Mariko is hesitant to offer help to others because she doesn't want them to feel pressure to repay it.	☐	☐
❾	According to Yoshi, refusals of help in Japanese are not as polite as they are in English.	☐	☐
❿	Living in Japan has had an effect on the way Juan asks others for help.	☐	☐

CREATIVITY   *Draw a simple* manga *based on the topic of this unit. It may be from your experience or your imagination.*

1

2

3

4

VOCABULARY
1. to incur
2. thoughtlessly
3. to burden ~
4. sympathy
5. superficial
6. euphemistic
7. to turn down ~
8. an extended period of time
9. humility

11 Interacting with Strangers

When you are sharing a space with people you don't know, do you smile at them? Make some small talk? Or do you ignore them to create a comfortable distance? There are a lot of cultural differences as to what is considered normal behavior towards strangers.

VOCABULARY 　　AUDIO 　　FOR TEACHERS

Part 1　You and Your Culture

WARM-UP SURVEY　Answer the following questions about your daily life.

Q1 Imagine you are riding an elevator to the 20th floor with someone you don't know. Which of these things would you do?

- make eye contact ☐
- nod in greeting ☐
- smile ☐
- say a short greeting ☐
- make small talk ☐
- look at your phone ☐
- ignore them completely ☐
- other: ....

Q2 Would you smile at these people if you passed them on the street?

	no	maybe	yes
• people you don't know	☐	☐	☐
• your neighbors	☐	☐	☐
• people you see every day	☐	☐	☐
• your classmates / co-workers	☐	☐	☐
• your teacher	☐	☐	☐

Q3 What do you think are appropriate topics for small talk with people you don't know well?

	appropriate	inappropriate
• the weather	☐	☐
• politics	☐	☐
• sports	☐	☐
• the other person's job	☐	☐
• the other person's hobbies / interests	☐	☐
• where the person is going	☐	☐
• news or current events	☐	☐
• your surroundings	☐	☐
• other:		

Q4 Where did you meet your friend(s) at university?

- same *zemi* ☐
- same class ☐
- same club / circle ☐
- same department / course ☐
- dormitory ☐
- friend of a friend ☐
- other: ....

Q5 How comfortable are you with the following ways of meeting new people?

	very comfortable	fairly comfortable	not so comfortable	not at all comfortable
• approaching someone yourself	☐	☐	☐	☐
• being approached by others	☐	☐	☐	☐
• being introduced by a mutual friend	☐	☐	☐	☐
• connecting by being members of the same group	☐	☐	☐	☐

VOCABULARY

1. to make small talk
2. to ignore ~
3. as to ~
4. strangers
5. to make eye contact
6. to nod in greeting
7. to pass ~
8. appropriate
9. inappropriate
10. surroundings
11. to approach ~

1. First, write your answers to Questions 1~5 in full sentences, giving reasons and opinions where you can.

Q1: What would you do if you were on a long elevator ride with a person you didn't know?

....

....

Q2: When would you smile at someone you pass on the street?

....

....

Q3: What do you think are appropriate topics for small talk with people you don't know well?

....

....

Q4: Where did you meet your friends at university?

....

....

Q5: What do you find is the most comfortable way for you to meet new people?

....

....

2. Ask the survey questions to several classmates and make notes of their answers.

	Q1	Q2	Q3	Q4	Q5
Example Name: *Misaki*	• *nod in greeting* • *looks at her phone*	• *yes: classmates* • *maybe: neighbors, teacher*	• *weather* • *news*	• *same zemi* • *same club*	• *most comfortable: being introduced (least comfortable: approaching others)*
Partner 1 Name:					
Partner 2 Name:					
Partner 3 Name:					

Now let's think about Japanese society and some differences between various groups. Write sentences using words and phrases from these lists.

elderly people		chat with
young people		stare at
men		avoid eye contact with
women		completely ignore
foreigners		strike up conversations with
people in rural areas		act politely towards
people in urban areas		make small talk with
		feel self-conscious among

1. I think that _____ are more likely than _____ to _____ strangers.

2. I have the sense that, in Japan _____ _____ tend to _____ _____ people they don't know well.

3. ....
....
....

How about you? Are you like most others in Japan, or do you have different views? Write more sentences about Japanese society, adding your own opinions or habits.

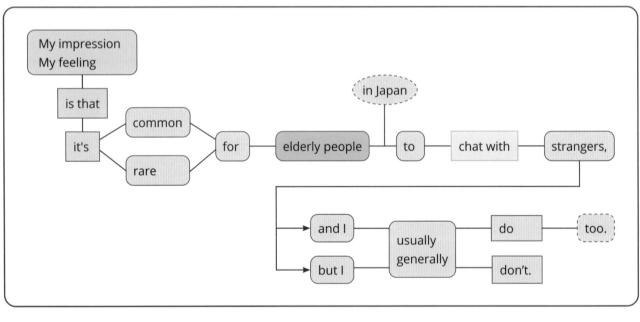

....
....
....
....
....
....
....

VOCABULARY
1. elderly people
2. urban
3. to chat with ~
4. to stare at ~
5. to strike up conversations
6. to feel self-conscious

People from a range of cultural backgrounds responded to the Ibunka Survey *on this topic. Here are a few of their responses for you to read and think about. You will find more in the* One Step Further *section.*

Q1 **What do you do when you share a space (for example being in an elevator to the 20th floor with one other person, or waiting in line at a supermarket) with people you don't know? Which would you feel more comfortable with: making some small talk, or ignoring that person? Why?**

Yuta
Japanese,
engineer,
has lived in Australia
and the UAE

❶ *I don't say anything. I act as if no one is there. I think it's the norm in Japan.*
🔊 11-01

❷ *I would feel more comfortable behaving as if that person didn't exist. If I don't know that person, I don't see a reason to communicate.*
🔊 11-02

Millie
Costa Rican,
yoga teacher,
lives in Japan

Jacques
French,
professor,
lives in Japan,
has lived in the USA

❸ *In France people usually keep to themselves, or might just say a word of greeting at most. But when I lived in the USA, I was surprised that people would always try to start up a conversation. The same thing happens when queuing for the supermarket cash register. Many American people soon engage in some light conversation. It seems like they feel a need to fill the silence.*
🔊 11-03

❹ *Once, as I was waiting in line to order in a fast food restaurant in Japan, an American man standing in front of me turned, saw me, and began to chat. This wasn't so strange for me, since in my country we sometimes make small talk with strangers while we are waiting. It felt pleasant to have a little conversation.*
🔊 11-04

❺ *But as we waited longer for our orders, he started getting more and more personal. He told me what he'd seen and done in Japan, what he did for a living, and then he started telling me about his family. He even got out photos of his children to show me. This felt too sudden and intimate. It was a little embarrassing to me.*
🔊 11-05

Brent
Australian,
lawyer,
lives in Japan

COMPREHENSION 1   *Read the responses and mark the statements **true** or **false**.*

	True	False
❶ Yuta feels that his behavior towards strangers is not unusual in Japan.	☐	☐
❷ Millie would probably ignore anyone who shared an elevator with her.	☐	☐
❸ Jacques found that Americans were usually very quiet when waiting to pay in supermarkets.	☐	☐
❹ Brent was happy to have a little chat with a fellow foreigner.	☐	☐
❺ Brent felt comfortable talking about his family with the man in the queue.	☐	☐

VOCABULARY
1. to act as if ~
2. the norm
3. to keep to oneself
4. at most
5. to queue
6. to engage in ~
7. to chat
8. sudden
9. intimate

Q2 Do you generally smile at people you don't know, when you pass them in the street, or on campus, etc? Why or why not?

Harry
New Zealander,
consultant,
has lived in
Thailand

6 *I think I do, probably because I _____ to be seen by others as a friendly person. I definitely _____ a smile if I get one first. I try my best to make myself open and _____ a welcoming mood for others.*

🔊 11-06

set
return
want

Yoko
Japanese,
English teacher,
has lived in the US

7 *No, I don't. Smiling at a stranger may be considered _____ in Japan. In my experience, people in North America are much more _____ to talk casually to strangers than in Japan. However, it does not mean that they will become _____ friends.*

🔊 11-07

likely
close
suspicious

Yves
French,
artist,
lives in Japan

8 *I don't _____ why anyone would _____ at strangers on the street for no reason, so I don't do it. If you did that in France, you'd _____ across as creepy.*

🔊 11-08

come
understand
smile

DISCUSSION | Which one of the survey responses on pages 71 and 72 was most interesting to you? Explain your choice, using the vocabulary in the box below. Then discuss your choice with classmates.

I found **A** Brent's response to be the most **B** peculiar. **C** I find it odd that ...

	A		
1	Yuta	5	Harry
2	Millie	6	Yoko
3	Jacques	7	Yves
4	Brent		

	B
1	peculiar
2	fascinating
3	surprising
4	relatable

	C
1	I find it odd that ...
2	I would say that ...
3	It seems to me that ...
4	I would never dream of ...

VOCABULARY
1. to set a welcoming mood
2. casually
3. to come across as
4. creepy
5. peculiar
6. fascinating
7. I would never dream of ...

Q3   **Did you find it easy to meet people when you were studying abroad?**

Megumi
Japanese,
interior designer,
has studied in the US

9   When I arrived at my host university in Berkeley, California, I was delighted because many people greeted me, smiled at me, and exchanged a few words with me. It felt so open and friendly. Later on, I realized that sometimes this was not as meaningful as I had imagined. But it definitely helped me to make friends there.

🔊 **11-09**

10   Nobody spoke to me at all during the first three weeks of my study program in Paris. I was shocked! I was expecting a warm welcome, but I just got ignored. But then one day I had forgotten my textbook and I had to ask some help from another student in my class. She was very nice and helped me a lot. That's when I understood that you have to take the first step in France. People won't talk to you just because you happen to be sitting in the same classroom.

Nobu
Japanese,
civil servant,
has studied in France

🔊 **11-10**

		True	False
9	Megumi realized that in the USA a smile is a clear sign that someone wants to make friends with you.	☐	☐
10	Nobu was able to make a personal connection with a French classmate once there was a reason to communicate.	☐	☐

CREATIVITY   *Draw a simple manga based on the topic of this unit. It may be from your experience or your imagination.*

1	2

3	4

VOCABULARY
1. delighted
2. to greet
3. meaningful
4. a warm welcome
5. to take the first step
6. to happen to ~

 *Here are some more responses from the **Ibunka Survey** on the topic of self-introductions. Let's examine them for underlying cultural trends. We can see that the language in many responses hints at two basic patterns.*

VOCABULARY   FOR TEACHERS

LOOKING FOR PATTERNS

CULTURAL PATTERN A: Blend in

In this cultural pattern, some people have a tendency to speak about things they have in common with others. Introductions are rather formal and standardized.

When introducing themselves, people tend to downplay their strengths and qualities. It is common to heap praise on others, and to deflect or even reject the praise directed at oneself or one's family.

CULTURAL PATTERN B: Emphasize uniqueness

In this cultural pattern, when introducing themselves, people have a tendency to focus on what makes them special or different.

Attitudes towards self-praise are varied, with people in some cultures being more assertive than others. However, speaking positively about one's own family is generally accepted.

*Read through the **Ibunka Survey** responses below. Highlight in one color the words and phrases that hint at Cultural Pattern A: Blend in, and in another color the parts that suggest Cultural Pattern B: Emphasize uniqueness. You can work and discuss this in pairs or small groups.*

1 Here in Japan, I've always found it <u>remarkable</u> how <u>formal</u> the greetings seem. Folks are bowing and using all these <u>honorific phrases</u>. It's kind of interesting. I prefer a <u>laid-back</u> casual approach.

American / male / professor / lives in Japan

1
remarkable
formal
honorific phrases
laid-back

2 In Japan I found introductions felt more formal, or sometimes <u>rigid</u>, than in the US, where it tends to be very casual almost from the beginning (depending on the situation and <u>players</u> involved).

American / male / journalist / has lived in Japan

2
rigid
players

3 I noticed that Japanese people like to mention their age when introducing themselves. They also sometimes mention their <u>blood type</u>!

Swiss / male / programmer / lives in Japan

3
blood type

4 When I was living in the US, I used to explain more about myself from the beginning, to match the atmosphere around me. Compared to Japanese people, I think Americans place more importance on <u>asserting individuality</u>. Living in a foreign country, I found out that I didn't know much about myself. Since then, I have come to know myself better. Also, I think that in Japan, we tend not to tell people about ourselves in a good way, <u>for fear of</u> appearing <u>boastful</u>.

Japanese / female / office worker / has lived in the US

4
to assert ~ individuality
for fear of ~
boastful

5 In Japan, my Japanese language ability has often been complimented, even if I only said "Hajimemashite" or "Watashi no namae wa ~ desu", and even when I was a total beginner. I found it a bit annoying at the beginning, but now that I am used to it, I just respond with a "Thank you!". More <u>tiresome</u> are comments on <u>appearance</u> like 'You have a big nose' or 'You have such long legs'. These are comments that would be taken as <u>outright</u> impoliteness in France, especially coming from strangers. It makes one feel <u>objectified</u> and not respected. <u>It is sort of like when</u> people here in Japan see a cat and exclaim "kawaii!". I am not a cat.

French / male / teacher / lives in Japan

5
tiresome
appearance
outright
objectified
It is sort of like when ~

6

I always look for opportunities to compliment others naturally. Going too far is not good, as it comes off as smarmy, but saying things honestly when it's _appropriate_ makes me feel good. When _giving compliments_, I try not to focus on superficial matters, like appearance, unless I know the person well. I've noticed that people here in Japan have no problem with this, _much to my consternation_. For example, I've gotten comments like, "Oh, you have gained weight since we last met!" Or, "Oh, have you lost weight?" There seems to be no problem with saying this here in Japan, but _it drives me crazy_. I've had to adjust to it over the years.

American / male / professor / lives in Japan

6
appropriate
to give compliments
to my consternation
it drives me crazy

7

I receive compliments from Japanese people a lot but for some reason I don't feel they are _sincere_. I don't know if that is because I don't agree with their assessment of my skills, actions or appearance, or if it is because I am personally unable to _accept compliments_. In Britain we are not good at accepting compliments. We always try to downplay them.

British / female / author / lives in Japan

7
sincere
to accept compliments

8

My kids and I once went to the house of my daughter's school friend. While we were there, the girl's parents kept saying how pretty my daughter was, and then they said, about their own daughter, while she was present, "Not like her, she looks like an old shoe". And the daughter agreed with them! She said "I do, I look like an old shoe." And she didn't, of course, she was actually very pretty. It's like the _aversion_ to _bragging_ goes to the other extreme. I never hear anyone say that their child plays a sport well, or the piano or anything like that.

Canadian / female / homemaker / lives in Japan

8
aversion to ~
bragging

9

I live in Japan, and sometimes I am not sure whether people really _mean what they say_ when complimenting others. Also, I feel it's common for Japanese people to compliment my Japanese language ability, even if I say nothing but "Hi." They don't mean to be rude, but sometimes I feel they are too quick to compliment. It's like if they aren't really thinking about me, it's just a _social ritual_.

Hungarian / female / research student / lives in Japan

9
to mean what one says
social ritual

10

When I am complimented, I try to be humble and _turn it into a laugh_ by making a joke. In Australia and the U.S., I have the impression that many people say "thank you" when they receive a compliment. I don't think that's very common in Japan.

Japanese / male / salesperson / has lived in Australia and the UAE

10
to turn ~ into a laugh

11

When I was working in Belgium, I got the impression that people who only talked about themselves and people associated with them were not _well-received_. I myself felt more comfortable with Belgian colleagues who were more _reserved_ in the way they spoke about themselves.

Japanese / female / career counselor / has lived in France and Morocco

11
well-received
reserved

12

I would say that I am rather modest when introducing myself. In the US, I find some people quite _extreme_ in how much they show of themselves. _To some extent_, it is nice to know some things about others, but I find people who _constantly_ brag about themselves quite annoying.

Japanese / male / student / has lived in the US

12
extreme
to some extent
constantly

EXPRESSION   Write a paragraph on the topic of introducing yourself. Include your opinions and reactions to the cultural patterns you found in these survey responses.

....

....

....

....

*Here are some more responses from the **Ibunka Survey** on the topic of sleep and rest. Let's examine them for underlying cultural trends. We can see that the language in many responses hints at two basic patterns.*

VOCABULARY   FOR TEACHERS

LOOKING FOR PATTERNS

CULTURAL PATTERN A: Give your all

In these cultures, it is admirable to work or study to your physical and mental limit. This means that you may sleep little at night, and rest wherever and whenever you can.

CULTURAL PATTERN B: Manage your energy

This cultural value is about getting a decent amount of sleep, and maintaining a regular bedtime and wake-up time, in order to be sharp and efficient for work or studies.

Read through the Ibunka Survey responses below. Highlight in one color the words and phrases that reflect Cultural Pattern A: Give your all, and in another color the words and phrases that reflect Cultural Pattern B: Manage your energy. You can work and discuss this in pairs or small groups.

---

①

Many Japanese people seem not to get enough sleep. It is amazing to see them falling asleep on public transportation at any time of the day, some even while standing up. Although my classes are very active (students have to talk a lot during the class) I've had a couple of students who <u>couldn't help but</u> <u>nose-dive</u> in the middle of an activity. This is something I've never seen in France.

When I ask them why they are always tired, they usually tell me that they have a part-time convenience store job that finishes very late at night, sometimes even in the morning just before class. From my point of view it's bad management of their sleep time, but I also get the sense that young Japanese people don't think that sleep is so <u>vital</u>!

French / male / teacher / lives in Japan

①
can't help but ~
to nose-dive
vital

---

②

In Canada a lot of people <u>are concerned about</u> how much sleep they get. There are occasional stories on the evening news or in the newspaper about the importance of sleep. From these stories, <u>it sounds like</u> people are not sleeping enough.

Canadian / male / employee / lives in Japan

②
to be concerned about ~
it sounds like ~

---

③

I have the impression that Japanese people have a very special relationship with sleep, as if they consider it a waste of time, but a pleasant waste of time. They sleep when they can (on the train, in the middle of a family <u>gathering</u>, at work, etc) but they have only very short sleeps at night. For me, Japan is the paradise of naps.

Irish / female / journalist / lives in Japan

③
gathering

---

④

My experience here in Japan is that people stay up too late, more so in the cities, though. In the countryside, <u>folks</u> tend to sleep better, and are more <u>in tune with nature</u>. However, the fact that many have hard jobs and <u>long commutes</u> means that sleep is quite lacking for many, as <u>is evidenced by</u> how often people sleep in public. It's interesting to me how <u>tolerated</u> this is

American / male / teacher / lives in Japan

④
folks
in tune with nature
long commutes
to be evidenced by ~
tolerated

5

As far I can remember, my parents insisted that I get to bed by a certain time, and that I wake up at a regular time. When I went to university, everything changed, and I became a _night owl_. Throughout my life I have remained aware of the importance of good rest. My wife and I bought top quality mattresses and _bedding_, seeing it as a way to support an important part of our lives. This kind of thinking eventually led me to use a smartphone app and _keep track of_ my sleep time. I find that doing so supports good sleeping habits.

American / male / teacher / lives in Japan

5
night owl
bedding
to keep track of ~

6

I was often asked why I wanted to sleep so much (between 8 and 9 hours a night). I always got the impression that Japanese people _associated_ sleep _with_ weakness or illness.

German / female / homemaker / lives in Japan

6
to associate A with B

7

Some young Japanese play video games, read or have fun until very late at night and have not created a routine for falling asleep and getting up at a set time. So when I ask them what they did the previous weekend, many students answer that they slept. Slept? Anything other than that? Just slept - all day long. That's _unthinkable_ in France! In my country we want to take advantage of the weekend to go out, to see family and friends, and have a good time. And we do get a good night's sleep.

Another aspect is related to noise. Japanese people seem to be able to fall asleep regardless of any _background noise_. Noise at night is _omnipresent_ in Japan, especially in the cities: people in the street coming out of bars and talking loudly, cars, bosozoku, etc. In France people would complain about these things but in Japan nobody seems to say anything. It's as if it doesn't bother them.

French / female / architect / lives in Japan

7
unthinkable
background noise
omnipresent

8

At first, I was surprised that it was _socially acceptable_ to sleep in meetings, especially the "smart sleepers"- the ones who could be instantly awake if a topic that affected their interests was discussed. Many of my students believe that the less sleep they have - especially before a test - the better they are studying. My belief is that they need to be _well-rested_, both to do their best in class and to learn out of class.

British / male / teacher / lives in Japan

8
socially acceptable
well-rested

9

I feel that many Japanese people do not have _respect_ for the sleep of others. I had to really _put my foot down_ to have my family respect my sleep. As children in France, we were taught to have consideration for other people, and not make any noise when a family member was sleeping or napping.

French / female / artist / lives in Japan

9
to have respect for ~
to put my one's foot down

10

Having enough energy is extremely important for me. For health and life in general, if you are tired, you _miss out on_ a lot of things and opportunities. And _on the contrary_, if you are well-rested you can fully enjoy your day and work efficiently.

Finnish / male / engineer / lives in Japan

10
to miss out on ~
on the contrary, ...

EXPRESSION Write a paragraph on the topic of sleep and rest. Include your opinions and reactions to the cultural patterns you found in these survey responses.

....

....

....

....

....

Here are some more responses from the **Ibunka Survey** on the topic classroom behavior. Let's examine them for underlying cultural trends. We can see that the language in many responses hints at four basic patterns.

VOCABULARY

FOR TEACHERS

LOOKING FOR PATTERNS

CULTURAL PATTERN A: Classes are interactive

In some cultures, much of the class takes place as "a dialogue between the teacher and individual students who raise their hands", as noted by the American respondent on page 21.

CULTURAL PATTERN B: Classes are teacher-centered

In other cultures, most teachers "do a lot of the talking and students just listen and take notes", as the French respondent indicated in his response on page 22.

Read through the **Ibunka Survey** responses below. Highlight in one color the words and phrases that hint at Cultural Pattern A: Classes are interactive, and in another color the parts that are suggestive of Cultural Pattern B: Classes are teacher-centered.

1
At university in Japan, we had both lecture-style and seminar-style classes, but most of them were one-way lectures by the professor. After that, I attended graduate school in the UK, for only one year so my experience is limited, but I felt that there was much more interactivity than in Japan.

Japanese / female / corporate trainer / has lived in the UK and France

1
one-way
interactivity

2
In Australia, students are encouraged to ask questions at all times. The teacher will also ask questions to the entire class and expect students to volunteer answers. I am led to believe that in Japan students are not encouraged to volunteer an answer unless they are directly addressed, and even then some don't.

Australian / male / sports coach / lives in Japan

2
volunteer
to be led to believe that ~
directly addressed

3
Canadian classrooms tend to be learner-centered and interactive. Students often work together to construct shared ideas concerning how to address a problem. Moreover, there are a lot of discussions and related activities that encourage learners to offer their opinions.

Canadian / male / teacher / lives in Canada

3
learner-centered
to address a problem
moreover

4
Yes, back in England classes were very interactive. They were teacher-centered and obviously it varied from teacher to teacher but in general we were encouraged to answer (and ask) questions, and often praised for doing so. I went to a lot of different schools (about 13!) and they were all like this. We also often worked in groups and were encouraged to present our work and findings to the rest of the class.

British / female / freelance writer and teacher / lives in Japan

4
back in England
to vary from ~ to ~
to be praised
finding

5
In Hungary, the atmosphere in classes varies depending on the type of school. University classes are based on listening and taking notes in silence. It's not really typical to ask questions, especially in lectures with many other students.

Hungarian / female / research student / lives in Japan

5

6
I grew up in Brittany, in the West of France. And I remember in high school, some language teachers would get really mad because no one was raising their hands to answer. A Spanish teacher once expressed how he felt puzzled, since he had taught in the South of France before, and he said that he was used to a majority of students raising their hands.
After that I went to university in Canada. Classes there were quite interactive, and I participated along with my classmates. The atmosphere was clearly more relaxed than what I had experienced in France.

French / female / language teacher / lives in Japan

6
mad
puzzled

> *To my mind*, not many classes are interactive in Japanese schools. I went to a Japanese junior high school for one year during my final year there. I don't *recall* any subjects where we interacted with one another, except for English class. In Japanese schools I get the feeling that students simply listen to the teacher and it almost feels rude to *interrupt* them with questions.
>
> Canadian-Japanese / male / student / has lived in Japan

7
to my mind, ~
to recall
to interrupt

LOOKING FOR PATTERNS

CULTURAL PATTERN C: Silence is OK
In some cultures, if a student remains silent after being called upon by the teacher during class, it is usually tolerated. This is perhaps because it is perceived as "the student is looking for the answer" or "the student doesn't know the answer". In these cases the teacher will usually move on to another student.

CULTURAL PATTERN D: Silence should be avoided
In other cultures, remaining completely silent after being asked a question by the teacher is considered rude, as seen in the French, Australian and Spanish responses to the *Ibunka Survey* on pages 23-25.

Read through the Ibunka Survey responses below. Highlight in one color the words and phrases that hint at Cultural Pattern C: Silence is OK *, and in another color the parts that show* Cultural Pattern D: Silence should be avoided*. You can work and discuss this in pairs or small groups.*

8

> During teacher training workshops, it is clear that the biggest, most common culture shock that foreign teachers experience when they begin teaching in Japan is the *classic* 'stuck in silence' situation, in which they call on a student to respond, but the student remains completely silent. To them, it feels as if they "threw a ball" to the student, but that student is "keeping the ball", refusing to *give the floor back* to the teacher.
>
> In trying to understand the students' side, I think that what matters most to them is actually the way their classmates look at them. There is an *invisible* but very strong social pressure to adopt a *hesitant* way of speaking.
>
> French / male / teacher trainer / lives in Japan

8
classic
to give the floor back
invisible
hesitant

9

> If a teacher called on me *specifically* during the class, I would try my best to answer the question. Remaining silent is not polite, at least in my opinion. If I didn't know the answer, I would guess, or tell the teacher that I didn't know. If this happened in a foreign language class, I guess I would at least use body language to show that I don't have an answer, like *shaking my head* or *shrugging my shoulders*.
>
> Chinese / female / software salesperson / lives in Japan

9
specifically
to shake one's head
to shrug one's shoulders

EXPRESSION

Write a paragraph on the topic of clasroom behavior. Include your opinions and reactions to the cultural patterns you found in these survey responses.

*Here are some more responses from the **Ibunka Survey** on the topic of the home as a social space. Let's examine them for underlying cultural trends. We can see that the language in many responses hints at two basic patterns.*

VOCABULARY

FOR
TEACHERS

LOOKING FOR PATTERNS

CULTURAL PATTERN A:
Socializing outside of the home

In some cultures, the inside of the house is seen as a private place that people outside one's immediate circle are not expected to enter. People feel more comfortable getting together in public places like cafes and restaurants.

CULTURAL PATTERN B: Socializing in the home

In other cultures, houses welcome guests on a regular basis because having people over for meals, drinks, etc. is considered an important part of friendship. In those cultures, it is important to keep one's house tidy and accessible enough that you can welcome visitors at any time.

*Read through the **Ibunka Survey** responses below. Highlight in one color the words and phrases that hint at Cultural Pattern A: Socializing outside, and in another color the parts that reflect Cultural Pattern B: Socializing in the home. You can work and discuss this in pairs or small groups.*

1

The first time I was invited to a party at a friend's home in Amsterdam, I took an expensive <u>store-bought cake</u>. But when I arrived, I saw that other guests were bringing simple things like a homemade pasta dish, or nothing at all - we were all students <u>on a limited budget</u>. I got used to that <u>relaxed attitude</u> after a while.

Japanese / female / teacher / lives in the Netherlands

1
store-bought cake
on a limited budget
relaxed attitude

2

The houses I saw in Ireland had a lot of <u>closets</u>. When I returned to Japan, I realized that the stuff I buy tends to pile up around me, because my home has very little <u>storage</u>. I can't have visitors just <u>dropping by</u> <u>without notice</u>, and if I wanted to invite someone over it would require a lot of preparation, so I <u>hardly ever</u> do it.

Japanese / male / company employee / has lived in Ireland

2
closet
storage
to drop by
without notice
hardly ever

3

In Australia, it is very common to invite people over for a meal and/or drinks. It's <u>not</u> such <u>a big deal</u> for most people.

Australian / female / consultant / lives in Japan

3
not a big deal

4

I often <u>eat out</u> here in Kyoto where I live. The quality of food and <u>hospitality</u> is really quite high, and the prices pretty cheap, so it's easy to find a good place to spend time with others. Sometimes I feel parties and events can be a little too <u>stiff</u> and <u>ritualised</u>, but eating out and talking with friends (and co-workers who become friends) is usually lots of fun.

Australian / male / translator / lives in Japan

4
to eat out
hospitality
stiff
ritualised

5

I usually <u>socialize</u> outside the home, that is, in a cafe or restaurant. I think one of the reasons for this is that inviting someone to your home means inviting them into a very personal and private space, so you have to be careful not <u>to give</u> them <u>the wrong impression</u>.

Japanese / male / banker / has lived in France and Canada

5
to socialize
to give ~ the wrong impression

6

I like having people over to my home to socialize. I love to cook and to <u>host</u>. Unless I was paying for my guests, I would <u>feel cheap</u> inviting people to a restaurant. If I wanted to see my friends, I would invite them to my home.

Australian-German / female / speech therapist / lives in Australia

6
to host
to feel cheap

7

Yes, here in Japan things are quite different from France; we don't often invite people to our house, even family. For example, when my Japanese wife's parents visit, we will pay for a hotel for them, even though they come from far away. They don't stay long at our place, either. In order to <u>adapt to</u> the local culture and especially to the wishes of my Japanese wife, I have gotten used to not welcoming people to our home very often. I miss it.

French / male / professor / lives in Japan

7
to adapt to ~

8

In my experience, Japanese homes are a <u>cluttered mess</u>, especially if kids <u>are involved</u>. Ours is <u>a disaster</u>, and I do not enjoy <u>having people over</u>. After a while, this "<u>who cares</u>" <u>attitude</u> <u>sinks in</u>, and it's just too <u>time-consuming</u> to bother with tidying up.

Canadian / female / homemaker / lives in Japan

8
a cluttered mess
to be involved
disaster
to have people over
"who cares" attitude
to sink in
time-consuming

9

I once visited a Japanese colleague without <u>pre-arrangement</u>. This happened by chance; I went hiking, got lost, and <u>stumbled across</u> her residence. She made me wait outside while she <u>tidied</u> the house - for about fifteen minutes-, before welcoming me inside. This was 35 years ago. I have not visited a Japanese colleague <u>unexpectedly</u> since then.

British / male / chef / lives in Japan

9
pre-arrangement
to stumble across ~
to tidy
unexpectedly

10

Tidying up the house does not seem as important as in France, since the space remains private and will not be seen by outsiders. French people often feel that Japanese homes are cluttered, not managed enough, and that they are not designed to be beautiful <u>on a daily basis</u>. In France, people look for beauty and <u>functionality</u>, but in Japan, I feel people are <u>preoccupied with</u> functionality and don't worry about beauty.

French / female / teacher / lives in Japan

10
on a daily basis
functionality
to be preoccupied with ~

11

Most Japanese houses I visited were often full to <u>overflowing with</u> stuff, just <u>piled up</u>. I guess this can <u>largely</u> <u>be put down to</u> the size of houses, or lack of storage options.

Australian / female / career counselor / has lived in France and Morocco

11
to be overflowing with ~
piled up
largely
to put ~ down to ~

EXPRESSION

Write a paragraph on the topic of having guests in your home. Include your opinions and reactions to the cultural patterns you found in these survey responses.

....
....
....
....
....
....
....
....

*Here are some more responses from the **Ibunka Survey** on the topic of club activities. Let's examine them for underlying cultural trends. We can see that the language in many responses hints at two basic patterns.*

VOCABULARY

FOR TEACHERS

LOOKING FOR PATTERNS

CULTURAL PATTERN A:
Clubs as places for fun

In some cultures, being involved in a club is seen as a break from studies, and usually limited to a few hours per week.

CULTURAL PATTERN B:
Clubs with rigorous demands

In other cultures, such as Japan, club life is quite intense in terms of demands on time and effort. This prepares members for their future life in society.

*Read through the **Ibunka Survey** responses below. Most are the impressions of foreigners who have had experiences of clubs at Japanese schools or universities, either as students, teachers or parents. Highlight in one color the words and phrases that hint at Cultural Pattern A: Clubs as places for fun or gaining skills, and in another color the parts that suggest Cultural Pattern B: Clubs with rigorous demands. You can work and discuss this in pairs or small groups.*

❶
I studied at a Japanese university on exchange for a year when I was in my second year. I was happy to be invited to join the basketball team, because it was my favorite sport. I also had the chance to practice my Japanese. After the first practice, a teammate took me aside. She praised my language skills, but told me that I should use honorific speech towards some of the other players who were fourth-year students. I was surprised because I'd been playing basketball longer than any of them, but I later realized just how important seniority in age is in a Japanese team environment.

Australian / female / marketing manager / has lived in the UK and Japan

❶
honorific speech
seniority

❷
Last year I joined my Japanese university's yosakoi circle. It was really different from the clubs we have in Hungary! Not only did we have three practices a week in different campuses, the attendance was mandatory! Once I skipped a practice, and it was really difficult to catch up with the others. That year's summer break was one of the busiest periods of my life. We had five-to-seven-hour practices four times a week and on the weekends, we went out performing.
Also, the Japanese students really spent all their free time (and sometimes school time) on the group's activities, which I couldn't really afford to do as an exchange student. I was always a step behind them and had difficulties making friends. Aside from that, it was quite a nice experience! I got to see how Japanese clubs operate and how much passion and effort the students put into them. I also had fun getting on stage and performing something amazing in front of actual audiences - that feeling made up for all the hardships I experienced.

Hungarian / female / hotel staff / lives in Japan

❷
mandatory
to skip ~
to catch up with ~
a step behind ~
to operate
audience
to make up for ~
hardship

❸
I think that the dedication and commitment of time to school clubs in Japan is extreme. Students devote themselves completely to something for three or sometimes six years, practicing before and after school and all weekend- but then won't spend any time studying! In most of Europe (except for the UK) there are no sports teams at schools or universities! If anyone wants to play sports, they join a club outside of school.

Swedish / male / educator / lives in Japan

❸
dedication
commitment of time
extreme
to devote oneself to ~

4

In New Zealand, a small number of students <u>dedicate their life to clubs</u> (usually outside the school or university). Many rugby players play in a school team, a local area team, and then a <u>representative team</u>. The difference is that this is only a very small group of people. Most ordinary students would never do this because they would fail all their classes!

New Zealander / male / professor / lives in Japan

4
to dedicate ~ to ~
representative team

5

I taught for two years at a Japanese high school. At first, I wanted to join the ping pong club to have fun and play with the students. Some of them chose this club because there were only three practices per week. Two or three hours on Tuesdays and Thursdays, and from 9 am to 2 pm on Saturdays. From 9 am to 2 pm -that's seven hours of club time ! The teacher who <u>supervised</u> wasn't a professional, so the students didn't learn any techniques. They simply played against each other non-stop. Some actually spent most of their time <u>clock-watching</u>!

I love living in Japan, but this is one area that I really don't feel comfortable with. Perhaps the boredom that students sometimes experience at clubs is supposed to prepare them for the boredom and <u>alienation</u> of the working world. Not <u>having a day off</u> and "suffering together," for example, is <u>the norm</u>. Absence <u>is frowned upon</u> more than poor performance.

French / female / teacher / lives in Japan

5
to supervise
clock-watching
alienation
to have a day off
the norm
to be frowned upon

6

My son loved playing basketball until high school, when the <u>demands</u> became too great. He decided he wanted to quit and I had to go to the school with him, where the two of us sat with the coach, the principal and <u>vice principal</u>, his <u>homeroom</u> teacher and a few more <u>attendees</u>. We were pressured for about an hour for him to stay in the club. I asked about his <u>academic results</u> and how he was supposed to study when he had to devote so much time to practice and tournaments. They told me he could study while he was on the bus going to tournaments and in between games. For me, the decision was not hard. If academics are your priority, then quit the team!

My son <u>was on board with</u> that. He quit. It was hard for him, socially ~ team members who had been <u>besties</u> no longer talking to him, for example, but he suffered no long-term consequences. <u>Truth be told</u>, I think it influenced him by teaching him that he doesn't have to bend to <u>societal pressure</u>, which can be so strong in Japan.

American / female / professor / lives in Japan

6
demands
vice principal
homeroom teacher
attendee
academic results
to be on board with ~
bestie
truth be told, ...
societal pressure

7

When I was in junior high school, I joined the tennis club because there was a rule that I had to belong to a club. I had to attend practice every day, and sometimes we had to go away on weekends for games, etc.

We had to treat our seniors with great <u>deference</u> and respect. It was the first time I had ever experienced such <u>hierarchical</u> relationships.

Japanese / female / career consultant / has lived in France

7
deference
hierarchical

EXPRESSION   *Write a paragraph on the topic of club activities. Include your opinions and reactions to the cultural patterns you found in these survey responses.*

....

....

....

....

....

....

....

....

Here are some more responses from the **Ibunka Survey** on the topic of communication in shops. We can see that most responses fall into two basic patterns.

VOCABULARY

FOR TEACHERS

LOOKING FOR PATTERNS

**CULTURAL PATTERN A:
Customers and staff on equal footing**

In some cultures, shop staff and customers communicate more or less as equals. The tone is rather friendly and warm.

**CULTURAL PATTERN B:
Customers treated as "royalty"**

In other cultures, the customer is treated with reverence, and staff generally use polite, impersonal language and behavior toward them.

Read through the **Ibunka Survey** responses below. Highlight in one color the words and phrases that hint at Cultural Pattern A: Customer and staff on equal footing, and in another color the parts that reflect Cultural Pattern B: Customer as "royalty." You can work and discuss this in pairs or small groups.

1

In Japan, where I grew up and where I live, the shop staff greet and thank customers very politely. Their behavior is often <u>impersonal</u>. Sometimes it's so polite and commercial that I feel it's <u>superficial</u>. However, in rural areas, there is more human communication. In France, where I've lived, shop staff are not always polite nor <u>pleasant</u>, but as a rule there is some eye contact and some "human contact". I feel that it's very warm. There are always greetings and thanks <u>from both sides</u>, and that's pleasant.

Japanese / female / interpreter / has lived in France

1
impersonal
superficial
pleasant
from both sides

2

In Japan, many foreigners face the <u>confusion</u> of, "Do I reply to irasshaimase?" In most of our own home countries there's a kind of obligation to reply to staff greetings, but in Japan, where shop staff are so very friendly and helpful, we are not required to respond. Though I spent some time in Japan, I always made a point of acknowledging the staff who took the time to greet me as I entered their store or section. Whether it was a smile, <u>a nod</u> or a konnichi wa, I felt that I <u>owed</u> the staff <u>as much</u>.

Australian / male / teacher / has lived in Japan

2
confusion
a nod
to owe ~ as much

3

To share an <u>anecdote</u>, the first time I entered the food section of a department store in Japan, I was shocked. I couldn't understand why everyone was shouting and making so much noise. I could guess that they were <u>bragging</u> about the freshness or quality of the food, but I didn't understand why they would need to do that.

Canadian / male / company employee / lives in Japan

3
anecdote
to brag

4

I lived overseas for a long time so I had <u>reverse culture shock</u> <u>upon returning</u> to the U.S. Once in a supermarket, the clerk asked, "Paper or plastic?" I wasn't sure what the question meant. She laughed and <u>rolled her eyes</u> and then held up two bags, a paper bag and a plastic bag. She looked <u>as though</u> she thought I was either a <u>smart aleck</u> or an idiot.

American / male / publisher / has lived in Japan

4
reverse culture shock
upon returning
to roll one's eyes
as though ~
smart aleck

5

In the States it depends on the store, but overall it's a lot more relaxed, and some staff do use humor to _keep things light_ and casual. I also think the staff will try to read the body language of the customer and their _initial reaction_ when they are spoken to, in order to see if they should _carry on_ a conversation or leave the customer alone.

American / male / teacher / has lived in Japan

5
to keep things light
initial reaction
to carry on ~

6

In China, I found that shop staff tended to be "clingy" and followed me everywhere, _pressuring me to buy_ something. They openly showed their disappointment when I didn't buy anything.

French / female / teacher / has lived in China and Japan

6
clingy
to pressure ~ to ~

7

In my experience, shop staff in China will try to actively push certain items, but customers generally ignore them and buy only the _items_ they want.

Chinese / female / college student / has lived in Japan

7
items

8

In Japan I felt like as a culture they are all about _hospitality_. I can remember the staff working at a McDonald's were just as _cheery_ and nice as the staff working at the nicest department stores. This isn't to say anything bad about McDonald's, but if you've been to a fast food restaurant in the States you probably found that not everyone working there is actually happy to be working there. From what I saw, Japanese people take pride in everything they do and want to do it _to the best of their ability_.

American / female / basketball coach / has lived in Turkey and Japan

8
hospitality
cheery
to the best of one's ability

9

First, the country where I grew up does not have a single unified culture. Even among people who belong to the same _ethnic_ or linguistic culture, behavior _varies_. As for interactions between staff and customers in shops, I think it really depends on the shop. At neighbourhood shops and _family businesses_, the interaction is more _personal_. At chain stores the interaction is more impersonal.

Canadian / male / teacher / lives in Japan

9
ethnic
vary
family business
personal

10

It's normal in France for customers to say hello to shop staff when entering a store, and say goodbye when leaving. The shop staff also do this, when they are not _engaged in_ discussion with a colleague. The service _varies_ a lot _from_ one shop clerk to another, but salespeople do not hesitate to give personalized advice and joke with their customers even if they are not _regulars_. I find it very pleasant.

French / female / teacher / lives in Japan

10
to be engaged in ~
to vary from ~ to ~
regulars

11

One of the things that was hard _to adjust_ to was the end of a purchase, and leaving a shop or convenience store. In America, the customer says, "Thank you," when receiving their _change_ or a receipt. That may be the end of the conversation, or the staff may say something like, "Have a nice day," to which the customer should reply, "You too." In any case, the customer speaks last.

In Japan, the shop staff always _see you out_ with a thank-you. If you _say it back_, they say it again. This can result in endless _loops_. Leaving without responding to them used to make me very uncomfortable. Now, I've learned how to say thank you at the same time _on my way out_ the door!

Japanese / female / career counselor / has lived in France and Morocco

11
to adjust to ~
change
to see ~ out
to say ~ back
loops
on the way out the door

EXPRESSION   _Write a paragraph on the topic of communication in shops. Include your opinions and reactions to the cultural patterns you found in these survey responses._

....

....

....

....

 ibunka SURVEY *Here are some more responses from the **Ibunka Survey** on the topic of romance and relationships. Let's examine them for underlying cultural trends. We can see that the language in many responses hints at four basic patterns.*

VOCABULARY   FOR TEACHERS

LOOKING FOR PATTERNS

CULTURAL PATTERN A:
Understanding through discussion

In some cultures, people believe that it's important for couples to discuss in depth the issues that they need to make decisions about.

CULTURAL PATTERN B:
Understanding without words

In other cultures, the common assumption is that people should be able to understand their partner's needs without words, and rely less on rational discussion.

*Read through the **Ibunka Survey** responses below. Highlight in one color the words and phrases that hint at Cultural Pattern A: Understanding through discussion, and in another color the parts that reflect Cultural Pattern B: Understanding without words. You can work and discuss this in pairs or small groups.*

1
Intellectually, I am attracted to the idea that partners in a relationship need to talk in order to understand each other. But when I think about it, maybe in reality what I really want is for my husband to guess my needs. It makes me feel loved. I think talking things over is necessary, but *upon reflection,* I don't share my opinions with my partner that often. As for older generations in my home country, I am pretty sure that they don't value discussion between spouses. In traditional Chinese culture, people are shy about expressing their needs.

Chinese / female / office worker / lives in Japan

1
intellectually
upon reflection

2
I think it's OK that my partner can't guess my needs, but she should be open to my opinions or requests. I believe that partners should always *articulate* their needs. I think my Japanese wife is more of the opinion that if you really care for someone, you should be able to *intuit* their needs. This might explain a *constant source of tension* in our relationship: I sometimes feel like she wants me to be a *mind-reader*, but I just want her to say what she wants. We somehow *muddle through*, and over time have learnt how to adjust to each other's styles.

American / male / university teacher / lives in Japan

2
to articulate ~
to intuit
constant
source of tension
mind-reader
to muddle through

3
My Australian wife and I always talk about things if there are any *issues*. We also share our needs with each other so that we understand each other *on a better level*.

Australian / male / sports coach / lives in Japan

3
issue
on a better level

4
I do think that "*unspoken*" understanding is a sign of a close relationship, but open and honest communication is *vital* in keeping it strong.

Spanish / male / university lecturer / lives in Spain

4
unspoken
vital

5
I am married to an Australian man. He's quite *expressive*, but sometimes when he's talking he tends to be too *long-winded*. I'm not stupid- he doesn't need to *spell things out* in so much detail. I think that being too *analytical takes* some of *the romance out of a relationship*.

Japanese / female / jewellery artisan / has lived in Australia

5
expressive
long-winded
to spell things out
analytical
to take the romance out of ~

CULTURAL PATTERN C: Having friends in common is desirable	CULTURAL PATTERN D: Having separate friends is more comfortable
In some cultures, people think that it's important that couples have mutual friends and do activities together.	In other cultures, many people think that it is easier and more appropriate if each partner has their own set of friends, since one's friends may not have much in common with one's partner.

Highlight in one color the words and phrases that hint at Cultural Pattern C: Having friends in common is desirable, *and in another color the parts that suggest* Cultural Pattern D: Having separate friends is more comfortable.

6

We do have some friends in common, but they are mostly my Japanese _partner_'s friends. It can be surprisingly difficult to get him to meet my friends.

Croatian / female / research student / lives in Japan

6 partner

7

Of course! Most of our friends we have in common, but not all of them. I want to see my friends _on a regular basis_, so if they were just my friends and not his, I would _end up_ spending a lot of time away from my husband. Plus, it's really fun to talk with him about people we both know.

French / female / teacher and translator / lives in Japan

7 on a regular basis
to end up ~

9

There are people I know who are family friends, but I don't think they would call us _mutual friends_. We don't have any friends in common because we went to different universities and work at different companies. It doesn't matter if we share friends or not. I don't think it's absolutely necessary to have the same friends as your _spouse_.

Japanese / female / counsellor / lives in Japan

8 mutual friend
spouse

10

No, not truly if I'm being honest. I have gotten to know the _key people_ in her life over the years, and do care for them, but I would not consider them "friends" _in the traditional sense_. In other words, I would not go out _on my own_ with these people. When I interact with them, my (Japanese) wife is almost always around. The same goes for her and my friends.

American / male / university teacher / lives in Japan

9 key people
in the traditional sense
on my own

EXPRESSION *Write a paragraph on the topic of romance. Include your opinions and reactions to the cultural patterns you found in these survey responses.*

....

....

....

....

....

....

*Here are some more responses from the **Ibunka Survey** on the topic of conversation and discussion. Let's examine them for underlying cultural trends. We can see that the language in many responses hints at four basic patterns.*

VOCABULARY

FOR TEACHERS

LOOKING FOR PATTERNS

CULTURAL PATTERN A:
Responding to questions with long answers

In some cultures, it is considered normal to give long and detailed contributions to conversation. These people try to put their conversation partners at ease by giving longer answers when asked a question, and speaking freely without being asked questions. Expressing yourself is seen as a sign of openness to communicate.

CULTURAL PATTERN B:
Responding to questions with short answers

In other cultures, people tend to give brief answers when asked a question, so as to give others more influence on the course of the conversation. The priority is to accommodate your conversation partner, in order to find common ground.

*Read through the **Ibunka Survey** responses below. Highlight in one color the words and phrases that hint at Cultural Pattern A: Responding to questions with long answers, and in another color the parts that reflect Cultural Pattern B: Responding to questions with short answers. You can work and discuss this in pairs or small groups.*

1
When someone asks me a question such as "Do you have a part-time job?", I tend to give long answers if I want to continue the conversation with that person. Talking about yourself often helps the conversation <u>branch off into</u> off into other topics, or leads to questions to ask the other person. But if I don't feel like continuing the conversation, I'm more likely to answer <u>dryly</u> and quickly, with an answer like "No, I don't."

Portuguese / female / lawyer / lives in Japan

1
to branch off into ~

dryly

2
When I am with my friends, I speak about myself without being asked questions, and also expect them to do the same even without asking. I am pretty good at talking, but not so good at getting others to speak. I feel like Japanese people around me would rather ask questions than talk about themselves.

Polish / female / homemaker / lives in Japan

2

3
In my case I tend to give long answers. Giving a <u>minimal</u> answer would feel to me like I'm not helping my conversation partner to speak.

French / female / translator and teacher / lives in Japan

3
minimal

4
If it's a friend from daycare, a neighbor, or someone with whom I want to have an <u>ongoing</u> relationship, I would try to give long answers. <u>Chit-chat</u> is fun and important in getting to know others, so while actively talking with others about all kinds of topics I try to maintain a <u>proper distance</u> by adjusting how much I talk about myself. However, if the person I'm talking to has a serious expression on their face, I would probably give short answers, because I wouldn't want to force them to talk.

Japanese / female / publishing executive / lives in Japan

4
ongoing

chit-chat

proper distance

5
I have lived in the US, and I am pretty sure that in that culture, replying to a question with just "Yes" or "No" would seem a little too short and plain. This kind of answer doesn't provide enough information to <u>lead to</u> the next question, so that <u>implicitly</u> indicates that you don't want to talk. But in Japan, short answers seem <u>preferable</u>. A long reply would feel <u>loaded with</u> words and too much information. I guess that because they are expecting a short reply, the listener might <u>miss the window</u> to reply, and could even get <u>offended</u>.

Japanese / female / jewellery artisan / has lived in Australia

5
to lead to ~

implicitly

preferable

loaded with ~

to miss the window

offended

CULTURAL PATTERN C: Disagreement is OK	CULTURAL PATTERN D: Disagreement is avoided
In some cultures, expressing contrary opinions is not taboo and can even be seen as "spice" for open, lively discussions.	In other cultures, disagreeing openly with one's conversation partners is considered uncomfortable and even rude, so it is generally avoided. As a result, abstract discussions tend to be rare.

Highlight in one color the words and phrases that hint at Cultural Pattern C: Disagreement is OK, and in another color the parts that reflect Cultural Pattern D: Disagreement is avoided.

6

I often feel uncomfortable with Japanese people when I talk about abstract subjects, because they quickly clam up so as to say nothing that could go against my ideas. This makes me feel like I'm forcing them to accept my point of view. I like to discover different points of view on a subject or a situation, even if I don't completely agree. It gives me a fresh perspective on the subjects in question.

Spanish / female / tour guide / lives in Japan

6
to clam up
to force ~ to ~
a fresh perspective
in question

7

For me to become friends with someone, conversation and discussion are important. I need to feel there is mutual trust between us, and that entails being able to broach almost any topic.

French / male / assistant professor / has lived in the US and Japan

7
mutual trust
to broach a topic

8

In Japan, where I grew up, in conversation we avoid disagreeing with other people and are always looking for consensus. This leads to "agreeing" with what others say, even when we really don't. In France, where I live now, disagreeing with someone doesn't necessarily frustrate them. It is simply part of the exchange, and an expression of the diversity of human experience. I particularly like this, because I am exposed to different views and this enriches my thinking.

Japanese-French / female / biotechnology consultant / lives in France

8
consensus
to frustrate
diversity
to be exposed to ~
to enrich

9

I rarely talk about abstract topics with people I am not close to, and I think that basically, my friends and family hold the same views as me. But if in the course of a conversation we found we have different views, we would probably change the topic.

Chinese / female / student / has lived in the US

9
to be close to ~
to hold the same views
in the course of a conversation
to change the topic

EXPRESSION

Write a paragraph on the topic of conversation styles. Include your opinions and reactions to the cultural patterns you found in these survey responses.

....

....

....

....

....

....

....

....

*Here are some more responses from the **Ibunka Survey** on the topic of parenting. Let's examine them for underlying cultural trends. We can see that the language in many responses hints at four basic patterns.*

VOCABULARY

FOR TEACHERS

LOOKING FOR PATTERNS

CULTURAL PATTERN A:
Parenting is centered on the child

In some cultures, many parents indulge their children, and often give them unconditional support (as seen in the Australian person's response on page 60).

CULTURAL PATTERN B:
Parenting is based on rules and manners

In other cultures, children are taught the social rules and etiquette of society in a rather strict way (as seen in the French person's response on page 60).

*Read through the **Ibunka Survey** responses below. Highlight in one color the words and phrases that hint at Cultural Pattern A: Parenting is centered on the child, and in another color the parts that suggest Cultural Pattern B: Parenting is based on rules and manners. You can work and discuss this in pairs or small groups.*

1 I was raised in a pretty strict family. I still hear my father's voice telling me to "sit up straight, don't put your elbows on the table". I feel like I've always been instructed in table manners, with rules like waiting until everyone was at the table before starting to eat, and only leaving the table when everyone was finished. I now live in Japan, near Tokyo. It blows my mind to hear my neighbor's child (who is about 6 years old) running and screaming around the house at 10 pm, sometimes even 11 pm, even on weekdays. I had to go to them several times to ask them to calm him down.

French / female / accountant / lives in Japan

1
to sit up straight
it blows my mind
to calm ~ down

2 A few things about parenting have surprised me while living in Japan. For example, we were at a friend's house and their child was jumping on the sofa, so my kids started jumping up and down too. I told my kids to get down. I said, "We don't jump on furniture." But the mother said, "No, no, it's okay!" I replied, "No, it is not okay. They can't jump on furniture." If other people's kids jumped on my furniture I would tell them off. And once my son opened someone else's fridge to get a drink. I told him off but the person said, "No, no, I don't mind." I said "I mind, it is rude and he can't do it." I also don't let other people's kids help themselves to things from my fridge.

British / female / writer / lives in Japan

2
to tell ~ off

3 When my children were in kindergarten and primary school in Japan, I was impressed by the sense of warmth and nurturing. I wish it had been like that for me when I was small.

Russian / female / housewife / lives in Japan

3
kindergarten
nurturing

4 Many American children interrupt their parents, and their parents let them, which I find very vexing. In France, if a child were to interrupt adults who were speaking together, the child would be scolded.

French / male / teacher / lives in the US

4
to interrupt
vexing
to be scolded

5 I think Chinese parents are strict because they believe that this is the only way to make their children study hard enough to survive the extreme social pressure. We have a large population, so competition is very fierce. My parents set an academic standard for me. I could fall behind a little, but it was not acceptable for my performance to dip below that line. It is true that as a Chinese student, if you fall behind several times, it is very hard to catch up again.

Chinese / male / manager / lives in Japan

5
social pressure
competition
fierce
to fall behind

LOOKING FOR PATTERNS

CULTURAL PATTERN C: Parents and children sleep separately	CULTURAL PATTERN D: Parents and children sleep together
In some cultures, children are made to sleep by themselves from a young age. This is to help them become independent, and also to allow parents to have intimacy as a couple.	In other cultures, small children are viewed as fragile beings who need to be nurtured and protected, so they sleep with their parents. The family generally sleeps as a group.

Read through the Ibunka Survey responses below. Highlight in one color the words and phrases that hint at Cultural Pattern C: Parents and children sleep separately, *and in another color the parts that show Cultural Pattern D: Parents and children sleep together. You can work and discuss this in pairs or small groups.*

7

My Japanese wife and I slept <u>alongside</u> our children for many years. We live in Japan, so it just seemed normal. I still remember the shock I had when, as a young couple, we were invited for dinner at a friends' place during a trip back to New Zealand for the summer. We had left our own daughter with my parents. Just before we started eating, around 7pm, my friend took his 2 year-old daughter upstairs to her room, and I went with him. I saw him switching off the lights, telling her good night, and closing the door. We went back downstairs and we adults had a wonderful evening, talking and laughing. For me, it was a <u>surreal</u> experience!

New Zealander / male / teacher / lives in Japan

7
alongside ~
surreal

8

I think a <u>preschool-age</u> child should be asleep by around 8 pm, and they should get used to sleeping in their own room as soon as possible, in order to develop a <u>sense of independence</u>.

German / female / writer / has lived in the UK

8
preschool-age
sense of independence

9

I think small children should sleep with their parents. Especially when they are only a few months old, it's better if there is someone <u>right there</u> to take care of them in case of any <u>emergencies</u>.

Chinese / male / student / has lived in Japan

9
right there
emergency

EXPRESSION

Write a paragraph on the topic of parenting and culture. Include your opinions and reactions to the cultural patterns you found in these survey responses.

....
....
....
....
....
....
....
....
....

*Here are some more responses from the **Ibunka Survey** on the topic of asking favors. Let's examine them for underlying cultural trends. We can see that the language in many responses hints at two basic patterns.*

VOCABULARY

FOR TEACHERS

LOOKING FOR PATTERNS

CULTURAL PATTERN A: Ask favors directly

In some cultures, it is considered respectful to ask favors from friends and acquaintances in a straightfoward manner.

CULTURAL PATTERN B: Ask favors indirectly

In other cultures, hinting at one's problem and waiting for friends and acquaintances to offer their help is considered respectful.

*Read through the **Ibunka Survey** responses below. Highlight in one color the words and phrases that hint at Cultural Pattern A: Ask favors directly , and in another color the parts that reflect Cultural Pattern B: Ask favors indirectly. You can work and discuss this in pairs or small groups.*

1
I think Japanese people tend to change their style depending on two things: what we're asking for, and who we're asking. For example, I can ask a family member or close friend for anything directly, but if the person I need a favor from and I have a less <u>intimate</u> relationship, I carefully consider the timing and how I should communicate even the smallest request.
Japanese / female / project manager / has lived in the UK

1 intimate

2
I think that Americans <u>have no qualms about</u> saying "no" to requests from others. So in a way, it's quite easy to ask for help. If they can't do it (or won't do it), they will let you know honestly. In the case of Japanese people, I feel I have to always be <u>cautious</u>.
Japanese / male / student / lives in the US

2 to have no qualms about ~
cautious

3
Living in Japan, I have had some <u>unpleasant</u> experiences with people who give gifts as an indirect way of asking for future favors. It feels quite uncomfortable to me.
French / male / teacher / lives in Japan

3 unpleasant

4
In Japan, I have noticed that sometimes when colleagues ask me for a favor there is an <u>unspoken</u> expectation that I do what is requested. Although the <u>phrasing</u> of the question may make it sound like there's a choice, the <u>subtext</u> is that I am expected to do it, <u>regardless of</u> how I might feel about it.
Canadian / male / teacher / lives in Japan

4 unspoken
phrasing
subtext
regardless of ~

5
I have the impression that Japanese people tend to avoid asking directly for help, <u>perhaps</u> because it makes them <u>accountable</u> to the person who helped.
British / female / biologist / lives in Japan

5 perhaps
accountable

6

Asking directly for favors is closest to my own experience. I appreciate <u>directness</u> and do not like being expected to read minds. But I think culture is better understood as the way different families within different <u>classes</u> live, as countries are just too big. Different families have different values, and sometimes it's easy to confuse what is normal to me as being 'Australian', when another Australian will have a completely different experience.

Australian / male / videographer / lives in Japan

6 directness
class

7

I was brought up in the West part of France, and <u>unconsciously</u>, I think I tend to give hints when I'm having a problem. My closest family members tend to ask favors directly, above all when it's something <u>practical</u>. But, when it's a much more personal matter, I think that in France, people would tend to talk about their problems, hoping to get offered some help

French / female / teacher / lives in Japan

7 unconsciously
practical

8

I think that in France, friends are usually eager to offer their help or advice if they feel they can; it's a way to show that you care, a mark of friendship. However, <u>unsolicited</u> advice is also common in France. You share a problem, and then some friends or people can have a tendency to give too much advice, <u>to the point of</u> being <u>annoying</u>. This type of personal <u>intrusion</u> is something I have never experienced in Japan.

French / male / professor / lives in Japan

8 unsolicited
to the point of ~
annoying
intrusion

9

From my experience in Japan, I think people consider it a <u>virtue</u> to <u>intuit</u> the help that their friends need, and just go ahead and do it without actually <u>consulting</u> them! I have been "helped by a friend" many times where the help wasn't actually what I wanted. I have learnt not to mention any problems I may be having, even to rather close friends.

From what I recall from my youth in Belgium, after hearing about problems I was having, friends would OFFER their help. That's a huge difference. When I returned to Belgium after some years in Japan, I noticed that there is actually a funny little dance that occurs in those cases. After the friend offers their help, it is common to first <u>turn it down</u> it, saying something like "No, that would be too much trouble for you". So then the friend insists, "Don't worry about it, it's really no problem", and this continues until finally the offered help is accepted. During this <u>back and forth</u>, the problem and its solution have actually been thought about by both people, so it's really rare to be helped in a way that doesn't match your actual needs. For me, this feels <u>straightforward</u> and respectful.

Belgian / female / teacher / lives in Japan

9 virtue
to intuit ~
to consult ~
to turn ~ down
back and forth
straightforward

EXPRESSION

Write a paragraph on the topic of asking and receiving favors. Include your opinions and reactions to the cultural patterns you found in these survey responses.

 ibunka SURVEY

*Here are some more responses from the **Ibunka Survey** on the topic of interacting with strangers. Let's examine them for underlying cultural trends. We can see that the language in many responses hints at two basic patterns.*

VOCABULARY

FOR TEACHERS

LOOKING FOR PATTERNS

CULTURAL PATTERN A: Interact with strangers

In some cultures, when people find themselves with strangers in a public space, they tend to smile and make small talk to feel more comfortable.

This usually feels quite "friendly", especially to people who are not familiar with that culture. However, simply smiling or chatting with someone does not mean that a relationship has started.

CULTURAL PATTERN B: Ignore strangers

In other cultures, when people find themselves with strangers in a public space, they tend to ignore them: no smile, no small talk. In this way, everyone feels more comfortable.

People don't communicate with strangers when there is no specific reason, because for them communication means the first step towards a relationship.

This can feel "cold" to people who are not familiar with that culture.

*Read through the **Ibunka Survey** responses below. Highlight in one color the words and phrases that hint at Cultural Pattern A: Interact with strangers, and in another color the parts that reflect Cultural Pattern B: Ignore strangers. You can work and discuss this in pairs or small groups.*

1
In the U.K, it is <u>fairly</u> common to acknowledge others, and you might even say it's a <u>social expectation</u>. This can be done with a smile, a nod, or even by saying hello when you enter an elevator, or if you <u>join a queue</u> and you make eye contact with someone. In supermarkets or shops, it is very common for the <u>checkout assistant</u> to start talking to you and it rarely feels <u>contrived</u>. This is something I sometimes miss about the UK. In Japan, I have found that a lot of people avoid both eye contact and small talk, unless you're somewhere where alcohol is being served.

British / male / translator / lives in Japan

1
fairly
social expectation
to join a queue
checkout assistant
contrived

2
Usually, on the street I would not <u>address people</u> I didn't know. So <u>I wouldn't mind not</u> talking to someone even if we were in the same space for a <u>longish</u> amount of time. But if someone addressed me first, then I would reply to them kindly.

Belgian / female / researcher / lives in Japan

2
to address ~
I wouldn't mind not ~
longish

3
<u>Let's say</u> I'm in an elevator with a stranger, and we're both headed to the 20th floor. If I am in a good mood and the person looks <u>receptive</u>, I would probably make a brief general comment on the way up. That is quite a long time to be in the same space as someone and not <u>acknowledge</u> them. I might at least smile or make brief eye contact to say, "yes, here we are, you and me, we are in the same space going to the same place."

American / male / freelance journalist / has lived in Japan

3
let's say ~
receptive
to acknowledge

4
When I meet <u>complete strangers</u>, I am rather <u>neutral</u>, but I smile and say a greeting when I meet a familiar face in my neighborhood or at work, even if I don't know the person.

French / female / teacher & artist / lives in Japan

4
complete strangers
neutral

5

If someone smiled at me in the street in France, _I would be like,_ "Do we know each other?"
French-Japanese / female / student / lives in France

5

I would be like, ~

6

In certain situations I smile at strangers, like _cashiers_ or moms who are with children who are _having a tantrum._ But otherwise I generally ignore them. Smiling is a way of communicating without words. If I don't feel the need to communicate, I keep a _neutral expression_ on my face.
Italian / female / engineer / has lived in Japan

6

cashiers
to have a tantrum
neutral expression

7

I don't understand why anyone would smile at strangers in the street _for no reason_, so I don't. But I feel quite comfortable talking and smiling, or even joking lightly if there's a reason for contact, for example when completing a _transaction_ with a shop clerk or _asking someone for directions_ in the street. When I'm back in France, I have also noticed that it's actually not uncommon for people to offer help to a complete stranger if that person seems to be in trouble.
French / male / artist / lives in Japan

7

for no reason
transaction
to ask ~ for directions

8

I feel that Japanese people exchange very few casual conversations with strangers. The fact that you use _formal language_ as soon as you speak to a stranger might explain this. It creates a kind of barrier. This is not the case in the States, because people are often _on first-name terms from the outset_, with people they meet in a casual situation, like at a party, or on campus. It makes it possible to feel "equal".
American / male / architect / has lived in Japan

8

formal language
on first-name terms
from the outset

9

Before living in Japan, I lived in Paris for three years. I thought French people were so cold at the beginning! I didn't get _a single_ nod, smile, or word from anyone. But in Japan it's even worse. I feel that people here don't even look at each other.
American / male / teacher / lives in Japan

9

(not) a single ~

EXPRESSION

Write a paragraph on the topic of interaction with strangers. Include your opinions and reactions to the cultural patterns you found in these survey responses.

CONTRIBUTORS

Authors

Stephen Richmond and Bruno Vannieu each have over 20 years of experience in teaching languages and intercultural communication in Japan.

Their collaborations include "Over the Wall of Silence - How to overcome cultural barriers when teaching communication in Japan" and the *Conversations in Class* textbook.

Stephen Richmond

Bruno Vannieu

Design

Véronique Dauce
(design and layout)

Éric Vannieu
(cover design)

Survey Database

Scott Rose
(design and development)

Mariko Nagano
(design)

This textbook was created at the Kyoto Impact Hub (https://kyoto.impacthub.net/).

The Impact Hub is a wonderful space that supports people working to have a positive impact on society. Thank you!

Acknowledgements

Thank you to the many kind people who participated in the Ibunka Survey and helped create the mosaic of intercultural experiences which makes up the bedrock of this textbook. We cannot thank individually all those who responded, but we are eternally grateful for your input.

We would particularly like to thank the following people:

Wes Armstrong, Yoriko Armstrong, Francesco Bolstad, Stephen Brewster, Alice Chavanne, Angélique Colin, Jay Crystall, Shawn Dennis, Itsuko Dohi, Yongru Duan, Bjorn Fuisting, Mari Futagami, Linda Gould, David Harrington, Nira Jayadevi, Yurika Kameya, Malaurie Koshikawa, Masanari Kuwamura, Louis Lafleur, Emilie Léger, Jon Letman, Patricia Muth, Takuro Nishimura, Yoko Noritake, Jeanette Pohlen, Vicky Richings, Tomoko Richmond, Taku Saito, Danish Sidhu, John Spiri, Michael Stout, Jerry Talandis, Janina Tomimoto, Tsuguyo Torikawa, Kevin Tortissier, Sachiko Yasuda, Natika Vannieuwenhuyse, Nina Vannieuwenhuyse, Pelaggy Vergnon, Xiyu Wang and Daojun Xu.

And super special thanks to Catriona Chalmers, Bruno Jactat, Catherine Lemaitre, Kazufumi Manabe, Stephen M. Ryan, Joseph Shaules and Jennifer Teeter for their crucial feedback and support, and to Jean-Luc Azra for a long and fruitful collaboration in intercultural and pedagogical research.

Finally, we acknowledge a great intellectual debt to Raymonde Carroll, the author of "Cultural Misunderstandings : The French-American Experience". Her rigorous yet illuminating approach to cultural analysis has deeply influenced this project.

Information and sample copies

Alma Publishing
info@almalang.com
Tel: 075-203-4606
www.almalang.com

Orders

**Nellie's English Books
(Shane Corporation Ltd.)**
shoten@nellies.jp
Tel: 03-6756-0064
Fax: 03-6756-0005
Individual orders:
https://nellies-bs.com/shop/

Ibunka! - Intercultural Communication in Everyday Life

2021年11月1日　初版第 1 刷発行

著者	Stephen Richmond, Bruno Vannieuwenhuyse
グラフィックデザイン	Véronique Dauce
発行所	Alma Publishing　株式会社アルマ出版
	〒606-8311　京都市左京区吉田神楽岡町5-41
	info@almalang.com
	TEL: 075-203-4606
販売元	株式会社シェーンコーポレーション　ネリーズ事業部
	〒101-0047　東京都千代田区内神田2-12-5
	shoten@nellies.jp
	Tel: 03-6756-0064 / Fax: 03-6756-0005

© 2021 Alma Publishing　ISBN 978-4-905343-30-1　定価:本体2500円+税
Printed in Taiwan